Novell® NetWare®
Troubleshooting the Network
and
Maximizing Performance

Dedication

To Uncle Joe, with love and gratitude.
Without you, none of this would have been possible.

—PR and SR

To my wife, Dena, who always believed
I would write a book. Here it is, dear.

—SL

Contents

Acknowledgments   *x*

Introduction   *xi*

A Short History of LANs and Novell   *x*
What This Book Has to Offer   *xi*
How This Book Is Organized   *xi*
Conventions Used in This Book   *xiv*

**1 Overview of Novell Menu Screens
and Command Line Utilities**   *1*

A Word about Novell's Menu Utilities   *1*
Novell's Menu Utilities and the Menu Utility   *2*
Accessing Menus and Selecting Options   *2*
Accessing the Help Feature   *2*
Submenus, Confirmation Boxes, and Information Entry Boxes   *3*
Exiting Menu Utilities   *4*
An Overview of the Menu Utilities   *5*
Command Line Utilities   *16*
    Supervisor Command Line Utilities   *17*
    User Command Line Utilities   *19*

2 Organizing Your Hard Drive   *35*

Concepts of Networking   *35*
What We Mean by Organizing the Hard Drive   *36*
    What Are Partitions?   *36*
    What Are Directories?   *36*
How to Organize Partitions and Directories   *36*
The ABC Company Example   *38*
What Is Filer and How Is it Used   *41*
    Filer and Volumes   *42*
    Filer and Directories   *42*
    Filer and Subdirectories   *45*
    File Information   *52*
    File Attributes   *54*
    To Copy Files   *55*
    File History   *56*
    Set Filer Options   *56*

3 Groups and Users, Trustee Rights, and File Attributes   *59*

What Is a User?   *59*
What Is a Group?   *59*
What Are Trustee Rights?   *60*
How Are Trustee Rights Assigned?   *60*
When to Use Syscon and When to Use Filer   *61*
What Are File Attributes?   *61*
Trustee Rights and Network Security   *62*
Adding and Deleting Users Using Syscon   *62*
Adding and Deleting Groups Using Syscon   *64*
Assigning Trustee Rights to Groups   *66*
Assigning Trustee Rights to Users   *68*
    Explanation of Trustee Rights   *71*
    Definitions of File Attributes   *72*
Command Line Utilities   *74*
System, Public, Login, and Mail   *77*

4 Login Scripts   *79*

What We Mean by Mapped Drives   *79*
What We Mean by Search Drives   *80*
Login Scripts and Messages   *81*
Login Scripts with More Than One File Server   *81*
System and User Login Scripts   *82*
Differences Between System and User Login Scripts   *82*
    Creating the System Login Script   *83*
    Creating User Login Scripts   *89*
    Copying Login Scripts   *92*
Creating, Deleting, and Editing Mapped Drives in Session   *95*
Creating, Deleting, and Editing Search Drives in Session   *97*
Login Script Commands   *97*

5 Security and Supervisor Options   *109*

User Security   *109*
    Account Restrictions   *110*
    Change Password   *113*
    Full Name   *113*
    Groups Belonged To   *113*
    Intruder Lockout Status   *113*
    Login Script   *114*
    Other Information   *114*
    Security Equivalences   *114*

      Station Restrictions   *115*
      Time Restrictions   *115*
      Trustee Assignments   *117*
   Supervisor Options   *117*
      Default Account Balance/Restrictions   *117*
      Default Time Restrictions   *117*
      Edit System AUTOEXEC File   *119*
      File Server Console Operators   *121*
      Intruder Detection/Lockout   *123*
      System Login Script   *124*
      View File Server Error Log   *124*
   What Is the Accounting Option?   *125*
      Blocks Read Charge Rates   *125*
      Blocks Written Charge Rates   *125*
      Connect Time Charge Rates   *125*
      Disk Storage Charge Rates   *125*
      Service Requests Charge Rates   *125*
   Accounting Reports   *125*
   How to Install Accounting   *126*
   How to Delete a Server from Accounting   *127*
   How to Deactivate the Accounting Option   *128*
   How to Set Charge Rates   *128*
   How to Calculate Charge Rates   *129*
   How to Change Charge Rates   *129*
   Account Balances   *130*
      How to Set Up Default (System) Account Balances   *130*
      How to Set Up Individual User Account Balances   *131*

6 Menu Utility   *133*

   Why Use Menus?   *133*
   Some General Information about the Menu Utility   *134*
   How to Make a User Menu   *134*
      Bob's Main Menu Text File   *135*
      Reusing Mapped Drive Designations   *145*
      Save the Text File   *145*
      Accessing Your Menu in DOS   *146*
      Accessing Your Menu from a Login Script   *146*
   Using Variables in Your Menu   *147*
   How to Control the Placement of Menus on the Screen   *147*
      Vertical Placement   *147*
      Horizontal Placement   *148*
   Changing the Colors of Your Menus   *149*
      Creating a Color Palette   *149*
      Deleting a Color Palette   *150*

Using Color Palettes in Your Menu   *151*
Color Palettes for Non-IBM Type Computers   *151*
Error Messages Relating to Menus   *151*

7   Printers   155

Concepts of Printer Sharing   *155*
What Is a Print Queue?   *156*
VAPs   *157*
Printdef   *157*
Setting Up Print Device Definitions   *157*
What Are Print Device Modes   *161*
Copying Print Device Definitions and Modes Between File Servers   *163*
Defining Forms   *165*
Printcon   *166*
Setting Up Print Job Configurations   *166*
Deleting a Print Job Configuration   *170*
Renaming a Print Job Configuration   *170*
Editing a Print Job Configuration   *170*
Selecting the Default Print Job Configuration   *171*
Copying Print Job Configurations   *171*
Pconsole   *172*
Attaching to Another File Server   *172*
Logging Out of Another File Server   *173*
Changing Your User Name on Currently Attached Servers   *173*
Print Queues in Pconsole   *174*
Listing Print Queues and the Waiting Jobs   *174*
Adding a Print Job to a Queue   *174*
Changing the Parameters of a Job in the Queue   *178*
Canceling a Print Job   *178*
Changing the Job Order in a Queue   *179*
Viewing and Changing the Print Queue Status   *179*
Viewing the Print Queue Servers   *180*
Listing the Queue Users   *180*
Listing the Print Servers   *180*
Viewing the Print Server's Full Name   *180*
Viewing the Print Server's ID   *180*
Creating a Print Queue   *181*
Deleting a Print Queue   *181*
Printing from the Command Line   *181*

8   Monitoring and Communicating through Terminals   189

Fconsole?   *189*
Broadcast Console Message   *190*

Change Current File Server   *191*
Connection Information   *192*
Down File Server   *196*
File/Lock Activity   *196*
LAN Driver Information   *197*
Purge All Salvageable Files   *198*
Statistics   *198*
Status   *208*
Version Information   *208*
Volinfo   *208*
Chkvol   *209*

9   Monitoring Through the Console   *211*

Nonprinter Console Commands   *211*
Printer Console Commands   *215*

10   Troubleshooting   *219*

Some Preventative Measures   *220*
Uninterrupted Power Supply   *220*
Duplexing   *220*
Tape Backup System   *220*
Preventing Data Loss Through Applications   *221*
Bindery Problems   *221*
Problems Opening Files, Copying Files, and Writing to Disk   *222*
Access Denied   *222*
Disk I/O Read Error   *222*
Failed to Create File   *222*
Failed to Open File filename   *222*
Fatal Copy Error Writing to Disk   *223*
Insufficient Disk Space to Write   *223*
Insufficient Space on Backup Disk   *223*
Memory Allocation Table Full   *223*
Missing or Invalid Command Interpreter   *223*
Users Are Accessing Blank Directories   *224*
Users Are Being Logged Out of the Network or Not Allowed
to Log On   *224*
Printing Problems   *224*
Other Problems   *226*

Index   *227*

Acknowledgments

WE would like to thank everybody who had a part in making this book happen:

Eli Hertz of Hertz Computer Corp., for generously providing the magnificent hardware used to set up and test ABC Paper Company's network.

Ken Cuite of Hertz Computer Corp. and Mark Leffler, an independent consultant, for reading the manuscript for technical accuracy.

Alan Axelrod of Hertz Computer Corp., for providing valuable technical advice.

Ray Pinon of Manufacturers Hanover Securities, for sharing with us every possible type of bizarre network problem that can occur.

Daniel F. Reilly and Lois Karp, for their encouragement and support.

Amy Gugig, our associate consultant, who put up with us and took over much of the office work and client support while the book was being written.

Paul Landsman, our lawyer and friend, who provided legal advice and multifaceted support.

Tracy Smith of Waterside Productions, Inc., our literary agent, for her assistance.

And a special word of thanks to our editor, Jerry Papke, for his patience and guidance.

Introduction

A SHORT HISTORY OF LANs AND NOVELL

It's ironic that the personal computer (PC) revolution has evolved the way that it has during the first decade of its existence. In the early 1980s, PCs were heralded as the ticket to independence from the corporate mainframe for most workers. A PC on a desk provided a user with unprecedented direct control over his or her computer environment. Instead of sitting in front of a dumb terminal connected by an umbilical cord to a behemoth machine governed by a systems manager, the user was able to choose, install, and configure software; select peripherals; and operate independently.

But a funny thing happened on the way to increased worker independence and control that reversed this trend. By 1986 many managers began to realize that connecting computers together into groups (called Local Area Networks, or LANs) was a better way to share expensive peripherals (like laser printers) and data that more than one worker needs to view or manipulate. The bottom-line benefits and return on investment achieved by a LAN has been so strongly promoted that companies that currently lack a LAN are viewed with as much disdain as companies that continue to use a hand-crank calculator.

Several visionary companies, such as Corvus, foresaw the value of connecting PCs together into a network at the dawn of the PC age. These companies, however, were financially and emotionally drained by the time the market was receptive to their message in the latter half of the 1980s.

In their place rose many contenders and after three years of competition, Novell has become the market leader. It is well documented that Novell leads the market in the installed base of current users and projected future market penetration:

- 450,000 software licenses have been sold since Novell began shipping netware (that is, 450,000 file servers).

- Approximately 4 million nodes (users) are currently using Novell.

- Roughly 70% of the Fortune 500 companies run Novell.

- Some market researchers predict that by 1994 Novell will have a 45% share of the market, IBM will have 15%, and Banyan, 3Com, and other vendors will share what is left.

Novell is a LAN Operating System designed to interface with the DOS market. As such, it consists solely of software and is system independent. Therefore, it is available for different computer platforms, including Apple's Macintosh, and engineering workstations such as Sun.

WHAT THIS BOOK HAS TO OFFER

Novell software, regardless of the version (there are different versions that vary depending on the number of users to be connected), is packaged with over a dozen diskettes and almost as many manuals. It takes knowledge and experience to install it properly and then many more weeks to begin to grasp the vastness of the software and master its commands in order to fine-tune the software and thus optimize work-group performance. Even experienced users and supervisors can find Novell complex to use and are sometimes baffled by the things that go wrong.

We feel that this manual will be an invaluable tool for LAN administrators. By logically coordinating Novell features, we give the user a tool to research projects without having to consult many different sections of the numerous Novell manuals. This book assists in troubleshooting by distinguishing between Novell problems and hardware/application software snafus. The turnaround time is improved, and the cost of third-party expert assistance is minimized.

This book does not discuss the installation of Novell software because this subject deserves a book of its own. Novell is designed to be hardware independent, and the installation process is hardware dependent. This book covers all the hardware-independent features of Novell Netware.

This book is written for Novell Netware 2.1x versions. For convenience, however, some references and troubleshooting tips have been included for earlier versions.

HOW THIS BOOK IS ORGANIZED

Although this book is written for supervisors and systems managers, it can be used by an inexperienced LAN administrator. It is not necessary to read this book in its entirety in order to use it. We suggest, however, that if you are not experienced in managing a Novell network, you should at least skim it. Each chapter is self-contained and deals with a specific Novell function. Each topic is discussed in the following manner:

- What does it do?

- Why is it needed?

- What is its function in the overall operation of the network?

- How is it done (including step by step instructions)?

- Are there other ways to achieve the same objective?

- Which way is better and why?

- Does it overlap with another feature? If so, cross-referencing is provided.

- Examples of a finished product and a line-by-line explanation of each example.

- Complete diagrams where useful.

We illustrate many concepts and commands by referring to the LAN setup at ABC company. ABC is the name of a fictitious company resembling one of our clients. ABC acts as an anchor for new information introduced in the book by serving as a real-life example of how a LAN was planned and configured.

Following is a brief outline of each chapter:

Chapter 1, Overview of Novell Menu Screens and Command Line Utilities, contains an overview of all Novell menu and command line utilities in addition to diagrams, a brief explanation of each main menu, and which features it covers. There is also a list of all command line utilities and how they are used. Cross-references are given to other areas, where each utility is covered in greater detail.

Chapter 2, Organizing Your Hard Drive, discusses partitioning, directories, and subdirectories. We suggest different ways in which hard drives can be set up to accommodate different needs and maximum network performance. Detailed explanations and diagrams of the Novell Filer utility are also included.

Chapter 3, Groups and Users, Trustee Rights, and File Attributes, gives definitions of groups and users, and explains their relationship to each other. Explanations are given of each group and user trustee right and how these rights affect network security. Detailed explanations and diagrams of Syscon, Makeuser, and Session are included.

Chapter 4, Login Scripts, covers definitions and detailed explanations of mapped and search drives and how each is used. We explain how to define mapped and search drives in Syscon and how to set up temporary mappings in Session. An explanation is given of differences system login scripts and user login scripts and how each should be used to achieve maximum efficiency.

Chapter 5, Security and Supervisor Options, explains the functions of a supervisor or supervisor equivalent in reference to setting up and maintaining a network, with emphasis on security problems and solutions.

Chapter 6, Menu Utility, shows the advantage of using menus with step-by-step instructions in how to construct menus and submenus. We also show how to reroute printers using the capture command in menu construction and how to change menu colors. Illustrations of different types of menus and submenus with line-by-line explanations of their construction are provided.

Chapter 7, Printers, discusses the concept of *printer sharing*; how and why printers are named; how to add printers to the network; and how to use Pconsole, Printdef, Nprint, and Capture to organize and control print jobs. We have given illustrations and line-by-line explanations.

Chapter 8, Monitoring and Communicating through Terminals, discusses the reasons for frequent checking of network performance. We show how to use Fconsole, Volinfo, and Chkvol to monitor the performance of a network. We have included numerous illustrations with line-by-line explanations.

Chapter 9, Monitoring Through the Console, explains how to use the console as a monitoring tool. We give explanations of all the commands, their syntax, and when they should be used.

Chapter 10, Troubleshooting, covers many of the problems we have encountered and how they were solved.

CONVENTIONS USED IN THIS BOOK

All commands have been put in uppercase for ease of identification. You may, if you choose, type them in in either upper- or lowercase. Italics indicates variable information that you **must** supply. Brackets enclose variables or parts of variables that are optional. If the variable is necessary to complete the command, Novell will either request the information or refuse to accept the command. Italic and bracketed variables indicate information that must be supplied if you are in a different path. Nested brackets enclose variables that are options in an option. If you include information within the nested brackets, you must also include the information in the outer brackets. A vertical slash between options means that you can use either one parameter or the other but not both. A right angle bracket (>) directs output to a file.

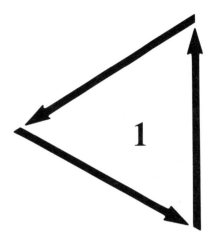

Overview of Novell Menu Screens and Command Line Utilities

MENU screens are provided with software packages to allow users to access functions easily. If a program is logically organized and menued, it is easier to use. Novell excells in this area. This chapter provides an overview of the Novell NetWare menu utilities. It also explains the Novell commands you need to access the various menus and, for the more experienced user, the short cuts around the menus using the command line.

A WORD ABOUT NOVELL'S MENU UTILITIES

Modern network management programs are complex. Novell Net-Ware is no exception. However, Novell has incorporated a system of pop-up menus, called menu utilities, so that access is logical and straight-forward. There are nine main menu utilities: Syscon, Session, Filer, Volinfo, Colorpal, Printdef, Printcon, Pconsole, and Menu. We will discuss each menu utility and its functions. We will also direct you to the chapter(s) containing full information about each utility.

NOVELL'S MENU UTILITIES AND THE MENU UTILITY

There is sometimes confusion concerning the difference between Novell's menu utilities and Novell's Menu utility. Novell's menu utilities are menu screens included with the software to provide users with easy access to Novell's functions. Novell's Menu utility is only one of Novell's menu utilities. This feature allows you to create your own menus to access the programs and other applications used on your system. Novell's Menu utility is covered in Chapter 6.

ACCESSING MENUS AND SELECTING OPTIONS

In order to access a Novell menu utility, type the name of the menu at the DOS prompt and press Enter. For example, to access the Syscon menu, type SYSCON Enter. The menu screen now appears on your monitor.

There are two ways to access a function. The first is to use the arrow keys to move the highlight bar to the function you wish to access, then press Enter. The second is to type the first letter of the function. The highlight bar will move to the function that begins with that letter. Then press Enter.

If more than one function begins with the same letter, you must type enough letters to distinguish between the functions. For example, the Available Topics menu in Filer has a feature entitled Select Current Directory and one entitled Set Filer Options. In order to access Select Current Directory without moving the highlight bar yourself, it will be necessary to type SEL to enable Novell to move the highlight bar to Select Current Directory.

ACCESSING THE HELP FEATURE

Novell NetWare's Help feature explains every feature in every menu. In order to access Help, go to any menu feature in Novell and hit the Help key. On most computers this key is F1. Some computers have a key labeled Help. If you hit the Help key once, an explanation of the feature you are currently working in will appear. If you hit the Help key twice, a listing of your computer's function key assignments will be shown. Key assignments vary from computer to computer.

SUBMENUS, CONFIRMATION BOXES, AND INFORMATION ENTRY BOXES

Each main menu utility has submenus. When you access submenus, they are superimposed on the previous menu screen. For example, when you access Syscon, the Available Topics screen shown in Fig. 1-1 appears. When you select Supervisor Options from the Available Topics menu, the screen you see in Fig. 1-2 is displayed.

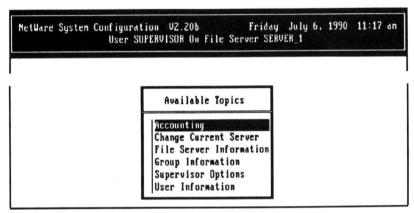

Fig. 1-1. Syscon main menu

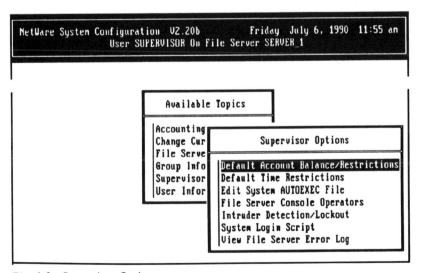

Fig. 1-2. Supervisor Options

Selecting some options will cause a list to be displayed. Lists differ from submenus in that you can add items to or delete items from a list.

Some features display an information box on the screen. These boxes require you to enter information from the keyboard. You can use your Backspace key to delete information in the box and type in new information.

At other times a menu utility displays a confirmation box with a message, such as Exit Menu or Save Changes. There are two choices you can highlight: Yes or No.

EXITING MENU UTILITIES

Novell has given you two options to exit from any of the various menu utilities. The first method uses the Escape key. When you are in a menu utility, pressing the Escape key will close the current active window, thus activating the menu on the next higher level. Keep pressing Escape until you have reached the Main menu (the highest-level menu) of the utility. When you press Escape again, you will get a confirmation box on the screen asking if you want to exit the utility. Highlight the Yes and press Enter. You must use this method if you have been editing any features in Novell NetWare. By pressing the Escape key a third time, a confirmation box will open. It will ask you if you want to save any changes. Highlight the appropriate answer—yes or no—you can then return to the DOS prompt.

For the experienced user, Novell also offers a second, faster way to leave the menu utilities. When you are done, press the Exit key. This key is different from one computer to another. Many IBM PCs use Alt-F10. To find the correct key for your system, press the Help key twice. This gives you a list of the key assignments on your computer.

Pressing the Exit key opens a confirmation box asking you if you want to exit the utility. Highlight the Yes or No and press Enter. The Exit key works from any level in the menu utilities. It will take you directly to the DOS prompt, stopping only once to ask if you want to exit.

The Exit feature is handy, but it does have its dangers: Say you have spent most of the day entering important data concerning the network operation. You want to save this work. *Do not use the Exit key*. Instead, use the first method to leave the utility—pressing the Escape key. This way you will be given a chance to save your work. If you use the Exit key, all your work will be lost.

AN OVERVIEW OF THE MENU UTILITIES

The following paragraphs summarize the functions of each Novell NetWare menu utility. Where applicable, each utility has been cross-referenced to the chapter containing detailed information.

Syscon

The Syscon, or System Configuration, utility is used to create users and groups, define trustee rights, work with file servers, and set up accounting functions. Access to each of these features is limited by a user's rights.

To access Syscon go to the DOS prompt, type SYSCON and press Enter. You are now in the Available Topics menu shown in Fig. 1-1.

Accounting   The accounting feature tracks charges for file server services for each user. For more information regarding the accounting feature, refer to Chapter 5.

Change Current Server   If your network has more than one file server, Change Current Server will allow you to change servers. Further information on this feature is in Chapter 3.

Filer Server Information   This feature allows you to view information about the file servers on your system.

Group Information   The Group Information feature allows the supervisor to create groups, add users, and assign trustee rights to a group. Users without supervisor rights can view this information. See Chapter 3 for more information about groups.

Supervisor Options   These options are available only to supervisors or supervisor equivalents. The supervisor or supervisor equivalent is the person responsible for smooth network operation. To do this, he/she has rights and privileges in every volume and directory. The following features are provided on the Supervisor Option menu:

Default Account Balance/Restrictions   This option allows a supervisor to assign default account balances and credit limits for given services. For additional information on this feature see Chapter 5.

Default Time Restrictions   This feature sets the default time restrictions for the system, to determine the hours during which users can log in. For more information regarding this feature see Chapter 5.

Edit System AUTOEXEC File   This feature allows the supervisor to edit the system autoexec file. See Chapter 5 for more information about creating and editing the system AUTOEXEC file.

System Login Script   This feature allows the supervisor to create a system login script. See Chapter 4 for detailed information about login scripts.

View File Server Error Log   This feature allows the supervisor to view and erase errors recorded in the system error log. A definition of system errors is given in Chapter 5.

User Information (for Supervisors)   By using User Information, the Supervisor or Supervisor equivalent can accomplish the following tasks:

- Set up individual account balances and restrictions for users
- Change a user's password
- Add and delete users on the system
- Add users to or delete users from a group
- Unlock a user account that has been locked due to intruder detection and lockout
- Create or edit a user's login script
- View the last login date, console operator status, and maximum disk usage allowed for each user
- Assign security equivalences for each user
- Assign station and time restrictions for each user
- Assign trustee rights for each user

User Information (for Nonsupervisors)   Nonsupervisor options allow you to see:

- A list of users defined on the current server and the groups to which each user belongs
- Your account balance
- The last time you logged in
- Your console operator status
- Your maximum disk space usage
- Your user ID number
- Your security equivalences
- Your station restrictions
- Your trustee rights

Each user can change his or her own password (if this right has not been restricted by the Supervisor) and edit personal login scripts. Chapter 5 has additional information on account balances, account restrictions, intruder lockout status, security equivalences, station restrictions, and time restrictions.

See Chapter 3 for additional information on groups and users and trustee assignments. Chapter 4 describes login scripts.

Session

A *session* is the duration between the time you log onto the network and the time you log off. You use the session utility to set up temporary mappings and to perform other "session-oriented" tasks. Session drive mappings are not saved when a user logs out of the system. The Session utility is not restricted by network security. All of its features are available to any user on the network.

To access Session go to the DOS prompt, type SESSION, and press Enter. You should now see the screen shown in Fig. 1-3.

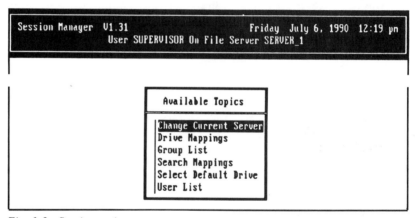

Fig. 1-3. Session main menu

Change Current Server   If your network has more than one file server, Change Current Server allows you to attach to and work with more than one at a time. To attach to an additional server, highlight Change Current Server and press Enter. A list of file servers will appear. Press Insert for a list of filer servers to which you are allowed to attach. Highlight the server you wish to attach to and press Enter. You will be required to type in your user name and, if necessary, a password. To log out of a file server, list the file servers to which you are attached, select the server you want to log out of, and press Delete. It is also possible to change file servers by using the Attach command at the DOS prompt. For more information on Change Current server, see Chapter 4. For information on Attach, see "Command Line Utilities" in this chapter.

Drive Mappings   This feature allows you to set up temporary drive mappings. Chapter 4 details the use of this feature.

Group List   This feature allows a user to send a message to a group. Highlight the group to which you wish to send a message and press Enter. Type a short message in the Message: screen that appears and hit Enter. Because you can also send messages using the Send command, see "Command Line Utilities" in this chapter as well.

Search Mappings   This feature allows you to set up temporary search mappings. Chapter 4 explains this feature.

Select Default Drive   Using Select Default Drive, you can change your default drive. To access this feature, highlight Select Default Drive and press Enter. The Select Default Drive list will be displayed. Now highlight the drive mapping you need as your default drive and press Enter. To change your permanent default drive, see the Login Script Drive command in Chapter 4.

User List   All users can access User List. With this feature you can view information about users who are currently logged on to the server. If you need information about users who are not currently logged on the server, use Syscon. You can also send a message to another user on the server. See "Group List" for instructions.

Filer

You use the Filer utility when working with volumes, directories, subdirectories, and files. A user's rights in Filer are governed by network security. To access this utility, type FILER at the DOS prompt and press Enter. You now have the screen shown in Fig. 1-4.

The following list briefly describes each menu option of the Filer menu. Chapter 2 has a complete description of this utility.

Current Directory Information   This feature provides information about the current directory. If you have the necessary rights, it allows you to modify features and trustee rights in the current directory.

File Information   This feature provides information about files in the current directory. If you have the necessary rights, it allows you to

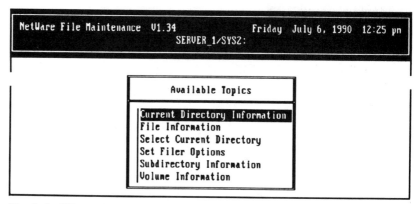

Fig. 1-4. Filer main menu

delete and rename files, as well as change file attributes. (File attributes are defined in Chapter 3.)

Select Current Directory   You use this feature to change the current directory.

Set Filer Options   You use this feature to change the default settings of the File Information and Subdirectory Information options.

Subdirectory Information   You use this feature to view subdirectory information; add, delete, and rename subdirectories; and change trustee rights in a subdirectory.

Volume Information   This feature allows you to view volume information for the current volume.

Volinfo

The Volinfo utility provides information about each volume on the file server. Volinfo is not limited by network security and can be accessed by any user. More information on the Volinfo utility can be found in chapter 8.

To access Volinfo, go to the DOS prompt, type VOLINFO, and press Enter. Figure 1-5 shows you what the Volinfo screen looks like.

Colorpal

Novell NetWare allows you to change the colors of all the menus in Novell, including user-created menus, through the Colorpal menu utility. Chapter 6 gives you the full details of using Colorpal.

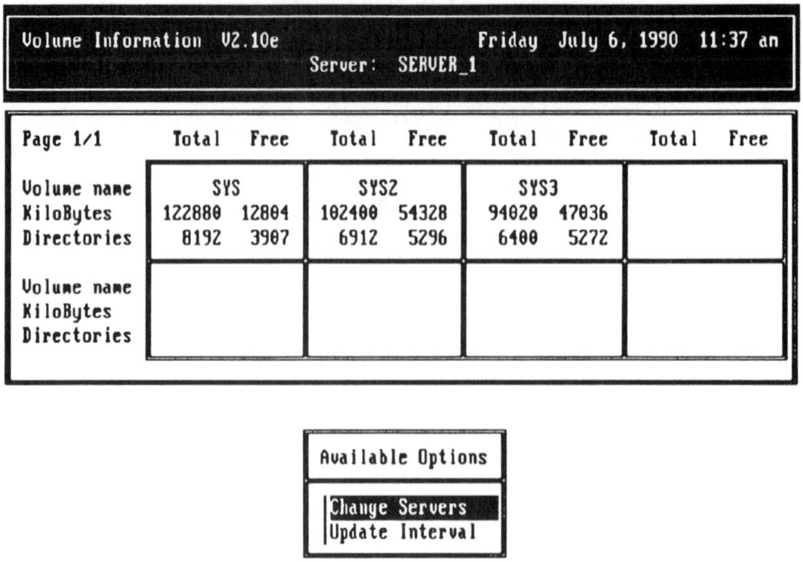

```
┌──────────────────────────────────────────────────────────────────┐
│ Volume Information  V2.10e              Friday  July 6, 1990  11:37 an │
│                        Server:   SERVER_1                          │
└──────────────────────────────────────────────────────────────────┘
```

Page 1/1	Total	Free	Total	Free	Total	Free	Total	Free
Volume name	SYS		SYS2		SYS3			
KiloBytes	122880	12804	102400	54328	94020	47036		
Directories	8192	3907	6912	5296	6400	5272		
Volume name								
KiloBytes								
Directories								

```
┌─────────────────────┐
│ Available Options   │
├─────────────────────┤
│ Change Servers      │
│ Update Interval     │
└─────────────────────┘
```

Fig. 1-5. Volinfo screen

To access Colorpal, go to the DOS prompt and type COLORPAL, then press Enter. Figure 1-6 shows the Colorpal screen.

Printdef

Printdef allows the supervisor to define and configure printer functions for all the printers attached to a file server. The supervisor can also create and modify forms for each printer. Nonsupervisor users can access printdef to view information about printers and forms. For information on the use of Printdef utility, see Chapter 7.

To access Printdef, go to the DOS prompt, type PRINTDEF, then press Enter. The Printdef screen appears as shown in Fig. 1-7.

Printcon

Printcon allows the user to set up configurations for print jobs. A printer configuration controls the way a job is printed. You use Printcon to create your own printer configurations. (You may also use forms created in the Printdef utility.) The supervisor can copy print job configurations from one user to another. For further information on Printcon, see chapter 7. To access Printcon, go to the DOS prompt, type PRINTCON and press Enter. Figure 1-8 shows the Printcon screen.

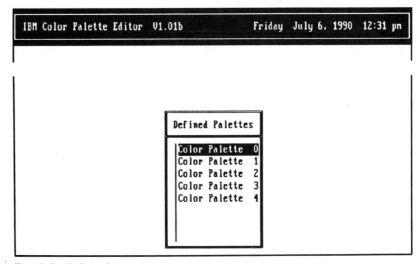

Fig. 1-6. Colorpal main menu

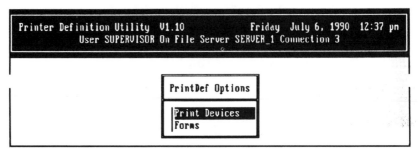

Fig. 1-7. Printdef main menu

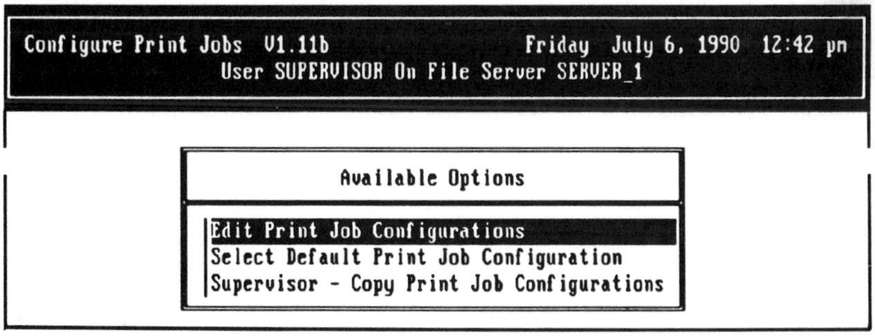

Fig. 1-8. Printcon main menu

Pconsole

Pconsole controls overall network printing. Access to its options is controlled by network security rights. Supervisors can set up and modify queues, and control the entire printing environment. Individual users can use Pconsole to view and modify certain features of their own print jobs. For additional information on using Pconsole see chapter 7. To access Pconsole go to the DOS prompt, type PCONSOLE, and press Enter. Figure 1-9 shows the Pconsole screen.

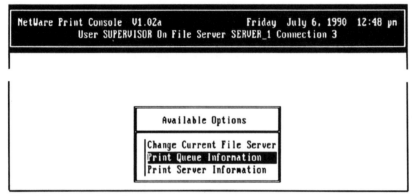

```
NetWare Print Console  V1.02a                 Friday  July 6, 1990  12:48 pm
              User SUPERVISOR On File Server SERVER_1 Connection 3




                          Available Options
                       Change Current File Server
                       Print Queue Information
                       Print Server Information
```

Fig. 1-9. Pconsole main menu

Menu

You can create your own customized menus with the Menu utility. Chapter 6 contains the information on creating your own customized menus.

Novell has a handy option for Menu. If you type MENU MAIN at the DOS prompt, you will have access by menu to all the menu utilities. With this feature you can move among the various menu utilities without having to go to the DOS prompt. To access this, type MENU MAIN at the DOS prompt. (Be sure you have a space between "menu" and "main.") You now have the screen shown in Fig. 1-10.

Makeuser

Makeuser is a Novell menu utility that, along with the Makeuser command line utility, is used to create or delete multiple users simultaneously. The Makeuser command line utility does this by executing a

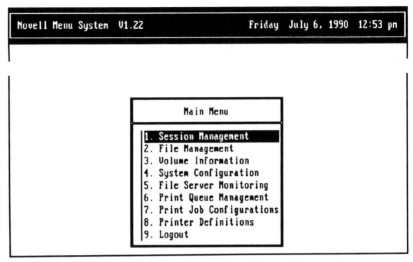

Fig. 1-10. Novell default main menu

special file called a USR file, a text file that contains the keywords used to create or delete users. The USR files are created and edited by the Makeuser menu utility. It is also possible for the Makeuser menu utility to execute the USR file just as though it were done from the command line. (This is not often done, however, as the process is more efficient from the command line.) For more information on the Makeuser command line utility, refer to Makeuser on page 75.

To create a USR file, type MAKEUSER at the DOS prompt and press Enter. The Makeuser menu is now on your screen. To begin a new USR file, highlight New USR File and press Enter. You now have a blank screen in which to create your USR file. The USR file is created by entering Makeuser keywords. The keywords allow you to set up defaults, such as login script assignments, password requirements, and accounting rights. Table 1-1 lists all the keywords with their definitions used in creating USR files.

Notes:

The Create or Delete keywords must always be included in a USR file.

All other keywords that you want to apply must precede the Create or Delete keywords.

You can create multiple users in a USR file. Clear or Reset can to used to mark the beginning of a new set of keywords in the same USR file for a new user.

Table 1-1. Makeuser keywords

Keyword	Definitions
#Account Expiration	Specifies when a user's account will expire.
#Accounting	Specifies the amount of accounting services a user can use. See Chapter 5 for information on accounting.
#Clear or #Reset	Starts a new set of keywords in the same USR file, after executing the keywords preceding Clear or Reset.
#Connections	Specifies the maximum concurrent connections a new user can have.
#Create	Creates users and specifies information about them. This keyword is required in a USR file to create a user. The syntax for using the keyword #Create is as follows: #CREATE [*username*]; [*fullname*]; [*password*]; [*groups(s)*]; [*trusteedirectory(s)*] [*rights*]
#Delete	Deletes users and information about them. This keyword is required in a USR file to delete a user.
#Groups	Assigns users to groups.
#Home directory	Creates home directories for users in a specified path. The user is then the owner of this directory. Specify full path.
#Login script	Assigns a login script to each new user. Specify full path of login script. For information on login scripts see Chapter 4.
#Max Disk Space	Specifies the amount of disk space a user can use on the network. Specify amounts in kilobytes.
#Password Length	Specifies the length of a user's password. Must be preceded by Password Required.
#Password Period	Specifies the numbers of days a password can be used before being changed. Must be preceded by Password Required.
#Password Required	Requires users to have a password.

Table 1-1. Continued

Keyword	Definitions
#Purge User Directory	Deletes the home directory and any subdirectories of the home directory owned by the user. Specify full path. See Chapter 1 for more information on Purge.
#Rem	Allows you to place remarks to yourself in a USR file—these remarks are ignored by the Makeuser command line utility.
#Restricted Time	Specifies time periods when the user is not allowed to log on to the system.
#Stations	Specifies which workstations a user can log in from.
#Unique Password	Requires a unique password when the password is changed.

Each keyword must be on a separate line and must start with the # sign.

If you use the same keyword more than once, only the last specified value will be used. The system will ignore all previous values for that keyword.

All fields in the keyword Create are separated by a semicolon. If the field contains more than one variable, i.e. more than one group or trustee directory, the variables are separated by a comma.

To extend the information for a keyword to the next line, put a + after a field or subfield.

Do not use the same username twice in any USR file.

If you do not specify a variable in any of the required fields in the Create command, insert a semicolon to indicate that the field is missing.

You may use a caret ^ to terminate a line.

Example 1

CREATE JOHN;;JOHNNY;EVERYONE; SYS:USERS ALL,SYS:WP ROS

This example creates the user John. The second semicolon indicates that a required field (Fullname) was left blank. His password is Johnny; he belongs to the group Everyone. SYS:USERS All means that he has been granted full trustee rights to the sys:users directory. SYS:WP ROS means that he has been granted read, open, and search trustee rights to the SYS:WP directory.

Notice that the Trustee Directories SYS:USERS and SYS:WP have been separated by a comma, not a semicolon.

Once you have assigned a group or directory to a user, all other groups and directories are subfields of the first and are separated by a comma.

Example 2

```
#LOGIN_SCRIPT SYS:PUBLIC/MAIN.LOG
#PASSWORD REQUIRED
#PASSWORD PERIOD 30
#UNIQUE PASSWORD
#CREATE JOHN;;JOHNNY;EVERYONE; SYS:USERS ALL,SYS:WP ROS
```

The first line of this USR file assigns the Login Script called Main.log in the SYS:PUBLIC directory to the user John. Password Required specifies that he must have a password. Password Period specifies that he must change the password every thirty days and Unique Password requires that the password must be unique (i.e. he must not have used it before).

Once the keyword defaults have been set, the Create keyword is used. In this example we created user John; the second semicolon indicates that the Fullname field was skipped; his password is Johnny; he belongs to the group Everyone; he has been given all trustee rights to the SYS:USERS directory; and he has been given read, open and search trustee rights in the SYS:WP directory.

COMMAND LINE UTILITIES

Although many of NetWare's features can be accessed by the menu utilities, Novell has provided the command line utilities to allow direct access to all options. There are two categories of command line utilities: supervisor and user. Supervisor command line utilities are located in the System directory and may be accessed only by supervisors. User command line utilities are located in the PUBLIC directory. They can be accessed by all users on the file server, although in some cases certain rights may be necessary.

Supervisor Command Line Utilities

The following supervisor command line utilities can be accessed only by supervisors or supervisor equivalents:

Atotal	Makeuser
Bindfix	Paudit
Bindrest	Security
Hidefile	Showfile

To execute a supervisor utility, you must either be in the SYS:SYSTEM directory, or you must map a drive to the SYS:SYSTEM directory and specify the drive letter before the command. Example: if you mapped SYS:SYSTEM to drive S:, then Atotal would be executed by typing S:ATOTAL from any directory.

Atotal

Syntax   ATOTAL [> *filename*]

Purpose   Atotal gives the supervisor a compilation of information from the system accounting records. Because this feature may fill up many screens, we advise you to direct the output to a file which can then be read or printed. For additional information on Novell's accounting feature, see Chapter 5.

Bindfix

Syntax   BINDFIX

Purpose   Bindfix is used to repair the bindery files NET$BIND.SYS and NET$BVAL.SYS. These files contain file server information about users, groups, queues, and accounts. For further information on Bindfix and bindery files see Chapter 10.

Bindrest

Syntax   BINDREST

Purpose   Bindrest is used to restore a previous version of the bindery files after running Bindfix. You can find more information on Bindrest and bindery files in Chapter 10.

Hidefile

Syntax   HIDEFILE [*path*] *filename*

Purpose   Hidefile assigns DOS Hidden and System attributes to a file. This hides the file during a DOS directory search. Files protected with Hidefile cannot be copied over or deleted. Chapter 3 has more information about file attributes. You can use the DOS wildcards (* and ?) to specify file names with the Hidefile command line utility. To make the file visible again, you use the command line utility Showfile.

Makeuser

Syntax   MAKEUSER *usrfilename*

Purpose   Makeuser is used to create or delete multiple users through USR files created by the Makeuser menu utility. You cannot use the Makeuser command line utility without USR files, which can only be created by the Makeuser menu utility. For additional information on using the Makeuser command line utility and the Makeuser menu utility, refer to Chapter 3.

Paudit

Syntax   PAUDIT [>Filename]

Purpose   Novell NetWare keeps a complete record of all accounting transactions in the file NET$ACCT.DAT. You can view all of the information by executing Paudit. This command produces large amounts of data. We advise you, therefore, to redirect this data to a file. You can view or print this data when needed. After the data is stored in a new file, you can erase the NET$ACCT.DAT file (but see the caution). The system generates a new NET$ACCT.DAT file to contain new information.

CAUTION: If your accounting or billing program utilizes the NET$ACCT.DAT file, do not erase the old NET$ACCT.DAT file until you are certain that it will not cause a problem with your accounting or billing.

For additional information on Novell's accounting feature see Chapter 5.

Security

Syntax   SECURITY [>Filename]

Purpose   Security checks for security gaps in the system by examining the bindery file and generating a report. Such weaknesses as users with no passwords, insecure passwords and other problems are brought to the supervisor's attention. Because the Security command can generate long reports, we advise you to direct the output to a file to view or print later. Further information on Security and users is in Chapter 5.

Showfile

Syntax   SHOWFILE [*path*] *filename*

Purpose   Showfile makes a file hidden by Hidefile visible again. Using Showfile removes the file's hidden and system attributes. The DOS wildcards (* and ?) may be used when specifying files in the Showfile command line utility.

User Command Line Utilities

The following command line utilities are located in the SYS:PUBLIC directory. They can be accessed by all users or, in some cases, by users with certain trustee rights in the SYS:PUBLIC directory.

Attach	Ncopy
Capture	Ndir
Castoff	Nprint
Caston	Nsnipes
Chkvol	Nver
Endcap	Pstat
Flag	Purge
Flagdir	Remove
Grant	Rendir
Holdoff	Revoke
Holdon	Rights
Listdir	Salvage
Login	Send
Logout	Setpass
Map	Settts

Slist	Tlist
Smode	Userlist
Systime	Whoami

Attach

Syntax   ATTACH *file server*[/username[;password]]

Purpose   Use Attach to connect to another file server attached to the same network. You may also use the Session menu utility (see above) to accomplish this task. You should follow this with a Map command mapping the newly attached server to a drive. Chapter 4 has additional information on the Attach command.

Capture

Syntax   CAPTURE *option(s)*

Purpose   Use Capture to redirect printing to a network printer. This is needed when applications do not automatically use network printers. The Capture command is followed by one or more options. Following is a list of the Capture options. For more information on how to use the Capture command and its options, see Chapter 7. You should also look at Endcap command in this chapter.

Show	*Keep*
Job=job	*Tabs=n*
Server=servername	*No Tabs*
Queue=queuename	*Banner=text*
Printer=n	*No Banner*
Local=n	*Name=text*
Form=n	*Form Feed*
Form=formname	*No Form Feed*
Create=filename	*Autoendcap*
Copies=n	*No Autoendcap*
Timeout=n	

Castoff

Syntax   CASTOFF [all]

Purpose   Use Castoff to suppress messages from other workstations when you do not wish to be disturbed or when a broadcast message would interfere with your work (for example, if you have an unattended job running on your workstation). Castoff will not suppress a message broadcast from the file server console. Castoff All suppresses messages from all workstations including file server console.

Caston

Syntax   CASTON

Purpose   Use Caston to re-enable messages from other workstations after suppressing them with Castoff.

Chkvol

Syntax   CHKVOL [*path*]

Purpose   Use Chkvol to check space usage for volumes on the network. This is the network equivalent of the DOS Chkdsk command. For additional information on the Chkvol command line utility, see Chapter 8.

Endcap

Syntax   ENDCAP *option(s)*

Purpose   Use Endcap to terminate capture to a network printer. The Endcap command is followed by one or more options. The following is a list of Endcap options:

Local=n	*Cancel Local=n*
All	*Cancel All*
Cancel	

For more information on how to use Endcap and its options, refer to Chapter 7. You should also see the Capture command in this chapter.

Flag

Syntax   FLAG [*path*] *filename* [option(s)]

Purpose   Use Flag to change file attributes. To use the Flag utility to change file attributes in a directory you must have Search and Modify rights in that directory. The following flags can be applied with the Flag command:

S	Shareable	N	Normal
NS	Non-Shareable	T	Transactional
RO	Read-Only	I	Indexed
RW	Read-Write	SUB	Subdirectory

If you use the Sub option with the Flag command, you change the attributes, not only of the files in the specified directory, but in its subdirectories, as well. You can modify file attributes using the Filer menu utility also. See Chapter 2 for further information on how to modify file attributes with Filer. You can find more information on file attributes and the Flag command line utility in Chapter 3.

Flagdir

Syntax   FLAGDIR [*path*] [option(s)]

Purpose   Use Flagdir to change the attributes of the subdirectories of a given directory. This command line utility is available with NetWare version 2.15 only. To use Flagdir you must have Parental and Modify rights in the parent directory. The following flags can be used:

N	Normal	S	System
H	Hidden	P	Private

Grant

Syntax   GRANT *option(s)* FOR [*path*] TO *user* | *group*

Purpose   Use Grant to grant trustee rights to users or groups. Chapter 3 has more information on the Grant command line utility.
    You can assign trustee rights with Syscon or Filer, also. Chapter 3 discusses assigning trustee rights through Syscon. Chapter 2 discusses assigning trustee rights through Filer.

Holdoff

Syntax   HOLDOFF

Purpose   Use Holdoff to cancel the Holdon command.

Holdon

Syntax HOLDON

Purpose Use Holdon to prevent other users from accessing a file while you are working with it. Your software package normally performs this task, but if it does not, use the Holdon command line utility.

Listdir

Syntax LISTDIR [*path*] [option]

Purpose Use Listdir to view the subdirectories of the current directory. You can also view the maximum rights mask and creation date. There are four options:

/S To view subdirectories and all subsequent subdirectories
/R View maximum rights mask
/D View creation date
/A View all

You can also view subdirectory information in the Filer Utility, which is discussed in Chapter 2.

Login

Syntax LOGIN [*server*][user [option(s)]]

Purpose Use Login to access a file server and begin execution of login scripts. If you do not provide your user name, you will be asked to do so. If necessary, you will be asked for your password also. If your system has more than one server, you should indicate which server you wish to log in to. You can only log in to one server. If you are logged into a server and log in to another server, you will be logged out of the current server. If you wish access to more than one server, you must attach to them. The Attach command is discussed previously in this chapter. All commands used in a Login script can be used with the Login command. See Chapter 4 for an explanation of all commands.

Logout

Syntax LOGOUT [*server*]

Purpose   Use Logout to terminate connection with one or more servers.

Map

Syntax   MAP
MAP *drive:*
MAP *drive:=directory*
MAP *directory*
MAP *drive:=*
MAP *drive:=drive*
MAP INSERT *search drive:=directory*
MAP DEL *drive:*
MAP REM *drive:*

Purpose   Use Map to establish temporary map drives at your workstation for the current server. For more on Map, see Chapter 4.

Ncopy

Syntax   NCOPY *filename* TO *path* [filename] [/Verify)]

Purpose   Use Ncopy to copy one or more files from one location to another on a network. Ncopy is the network version of the DOS Copy command. Although the DOS Copy command can be used, Ncopy works more efficiently in a network environment. If you use the /Verify option, Ncopy verifies that the original file and the copied file are identical. You can use DOS wildcards (* and ?) with Ncopy.

Ndir

Syntax   NDIR [*path*] [Filename [option(s)]]

Purpose   Use Ndir to get the following information about files in a directory or subdirectory:

- The file names
- Number of bytes in a file
- Date and time files were last updated
- Date files were last accessed
- Date files were last archived

- Date files were created
- File attributes
- File owners
- Files created by a Macintosh

Use Ndir to search and view the following information about subdirectories:

- Subdirectory names
- Date subdirectories were created
- Subdirectories' maximum rights mask
- Your effective rights in subdirectories
- Owner of the subdirectories

You can use the following options with the Ndir command. (Note: The DOS wild cards * and ? can be used.)

Basic File Information

FILENAME [not]=*file*

    Show all files [except those] related by file name.

        Example: NDIR *.LTR

                will show all files with an *.LTR extension.

                NDIR *.* FILENAME NOT EQUAL *.LTR

                will show all files except those with an *.LTR extension.

OWNER [NOT]=*name*

    Show all files in a directory [except those] created by same user.

ACCESS [NOT] *BEFORE* | = | *AFTER mm-dd-yy*

    Show all files in a directory [except those] last accessed on, before, or after said date.

UPDATE [NOT] *BEFORE* | = | *AFTER mm-dd-yy*

    Show all files in a directory [except those] last updated on, before, or after said date.

CREATE [NOT] *BEFORE* | = | *AFTER mm-dd-yy*

Shows all files in a directory [except those] created on, before, or after said date.

SIZE [NOT] *GREATER THAN* | = | *LESS THAN nnn*

Shows all files in a directory [except those] with byte sizes greater than, equal to, or less than said value.

[NOT] SYSTEM

Shows all files in a directory [except those] with System file attribute.

[NOT] HIDDEN

Shows all files in a directory [except those] with Hidden file attribute.

[NOT] MODIFIED

Shows all files in a directory [except those] with Modified file attribute.

[NOT] EXECUTE ONLY

Shows all files in a directory [except those] with Execute-only file attribute.

[NOT] SHAREABLE

Shows all files in a directory [except those] with Shareable file attribute.

[NOT] READ ONLY

Shows all files in a directory [except those] with Read-only file attribute.

[NOT] READ WRITE

Shows all files in a directory [except those] with Read-write file attribute.

[NOT] INDEXED

Shows all files in a directory [except those] with Indexed file attribute.

[NOT] TRANSACTIONAL

Shows all files in a directory [except those] with Transactional file attribute.

Sort File Information

[REVERSE] SORT FILENAME

Shows all files in a directory in [reverse] alphabetical order.

[REVERSE] SORT OWNER

Shows all files in a directory by owner name in [reverse] alphabetical order.

[REVERSE] SORT ACCESS

Shows all files in a directory by last accessed date from earliest date to latest [or latest to earliest].

[REVERSE] SORT UPDATE

Shows all files in a directory by last update date from earliest to latest [or latest to earliest].

[REVERSE] SORT CREATE

Shows all files in a directory by creation date from earliest to latest [or latest to earliest].

[REVERSE] SORT SIZE

Shows all files in a directory by size from smallest to largest [or largest to smallest].

View-Only Information

FILES ONLY

Shows only the files in a given directory.

DIRECTORIES ONLY

Shows only the subdirectories in a given directory.

MAC

Shows only Macintosh files and subdirectories.

SUB

Shows all subdirectories and lower level subdirectories.

BRIEF

Shows only the size and last update of each file in a directory.

Archiving Information

BACKUP

Shows only last modified date and last archived date of all files in a directory. All other information will be omitted. Unless Wide option is used, the files are shown in Backup display.

WIDE

Use with archiving information options to show all default information rather than just Backup display.

[NOT] ARCHIVED

Shows all files that have [not] been archived.

ARCHIVED DATE *BEFORE* | = | *AFTER mm-dd-yy*

Shows all files archived before, on or after said date.

CHANGED

Shows all files updated since last archive and all files never archived.

[NOT] ARCHIVED BIT

Shows all files archived with DOS archive bit.

[NOT] TOUCHED

Shows all files that have [not] been modified since last archive.

HELP

Displays help screen showing command format and options for Ndir command line utility.

For additional information on files, directories, and subdirectories, see the Filer Utility in Chapter 2. For additional information on rights and attributes, see Chapter 3.

Nprint

Syntax   NPRINT [*filename*] [option(s)]

Purpose   Use Nprint to send DOS text files to a network printer. The NPRINT options are the same as the Capture command line utility options. For additional information on Nprint and Capture, see Chapter 7.

Nsnipes

Syntax   NSNIPES or NCSNIPES

Purpose   Nsnipes is a network game that can be played by one or more users on a network. Nsnipes is the monochrome version and Ncsnipes is the color version. To exit the game press Ctrl-Break. Instructions for playing Nsnipes may be found in Novell NetWare "Command Line Utilities" manual.

Nver

Syntax   NVER

Purpose   Nver yields information about your Netbios, Ipx, Spx, LAN driver, shell, workstation operating system, and file server operating system. This command is only available with NetWare 2.15.

Pstat

Syntax   PSTAT

Purpose   Pstat gives you the following information about the network printers on the current server:

- Printer number
- On-line status
- Whether the printer is Active or Stopped
- Form number and name

For additional information on network printing, see Chapter 7.

Purge

Syntax   PURGE

Purpose   Purge frees directory entries by breaking the attachment between the file and its directory entry. Merely erasing or deleting a file does not accomplish this. The Purge command renders all previously erased file irrecoverable. The Novell Salvage command will not restore any file deleted by Purge.

Remove

Syntax   REMOVE [USER] *user* | [GROUP] *group* FROM [*path*]

Purpose   Use Remove to remove a user or group from the trustee list of a directory. To use Remove you must have Parental rights in the given directory. For additional information on Remove see Chapter 3.

You can remove groups and users from the trustee list of a directory by using the Syscon and Filer menu utilities, also. Chapter 3 discusses Syscon in detail. The filer utility is covered in Chapter 2.

Rendir

Syntax   RENDIR [*path*] *directory* TO [*path*] *directory*

Purpose   Rendir is used to rename directories and subdirectories. To use Rendir you must have Parental and Modify rights in the given directory or subdirectory. You can rename directories and subdirectories by using Filer, discussed in Chapter 2.

Revoke

Syntax: REVOKE *option(s)* FOR [*path*] FROM *user* | *group*

Purpose   Revoke removes trustee rights from a user or group in a directory. Revoke requires you to have Parental rights in the given directory. For additional information on Revoke, see Chapter 3. Trustee rights can also be revoked by using the Syscon and Filer menu utilities. (Syscon use is discussed in Chapter 3; Filer, in Chapter 2.)

Rights

Syntax   RIGHTS [*path*]

Purpose   Use Rights to view your rights in a directory.

Salvage

Syntax   SALVAGE [*path*]

Purpose   You can use Salvage to recover an erased file or files. The following requirements apply:

- Do not log out of your server.

- Do not create or erase any additional files on the volume from which your file was erased.

- Do not issue a Purge command.
- The Salvage command must be issued on the same workstation used to delete the file.

Send

Syntax   SEND "message" [TO] [server/] [user(s)][group(s)]

Purpose   Use Send to send short messages to other users or groups on the network. These messages appear at the bottom of the recipients' monitors' screens. The variable message in the syntax line represents any string up to 45 characters long. The Session utility can also be used to send messages to users and groups.

Setpass

Syntax   SETPASS [*server*]

Purpose   Use Setpass to change your own password. This command can only be used by users whose right to change their own passwords has not been restricted. For further information on passwords, see Syscon in Chapter 5.

Settts

Syntax   SETTTS [*logical level*[*physical level*]]

Purpose   Use Settts to ensure that the Transaction Tracking System (TTS) within SFT NetWare is properly initialized to work with certain application software. Each level can be reset with a number from 1 through 255. You should use the Setts utility only if you understand how the TTS works. For more information on TTS, consult your Novell "SFT/ Advanced Netware 286 Maintenance" manual.

Slist

Syntax   SLIST

Purpose   Use Slist to view a list of file servers running on your network or internetwork.

Smode

Syntax   SMODE [*path*] | *filename* [option]

Purpose   Use Smode to view or assign a search mode to an executable (.EXE or .COM) file. Options are represented by numbers 0 through 7.

0 No search instructions.

1 The file will search the path specified within the file itself, or, if a path is not specified, the file will search the default directory and all search drives.

2 The file will search only the default directory.

3 The file will only search the path specified within the file itself. If a path is not specified and the file opens data files Read-Only, the file will search the default directory and all search drives.

4 Reserved

5 The file will search the default directory and all search drives.

6 Reserved

7 If the file opens data files Read-Only the file will search the default directory and all search drives.

Systime

Syntax   SYSTIME [*server*]

Purpose   Use Systime to view the day of the week, date and time set on any server on your network. This also synchronizes the settings of the viewed server with your workstation.

Tlist

Syntax   TLIST [*path*[users | groups]]

Purpose   Use Tlist to view the trustee list for a directory. You must have Parental rights in the given directory to use Tlist. You can view this information in Filer. For more information on Filer, see Chapter 2.

Userlist

Syntax   USERLIST [*server*] [*user*] [/A]

Purpose   Use Userlist to see a list of users on a given server. Using the /A option gives you each user's connection number, login time, network address and node address.

Whoami

Syntax   WHOAMI [server] [option]

Purpose   Whoami gives you the following information about you and your relation to the network:

- Which servers you are attached to
- Your user name on each server
- Your login date and time for each server
- Group affiliations on each server
- Security equivalences on each server
- Effective rights on the network

The following options are available:

/G   Groups
/S   Security
/R   Rights
/A   All

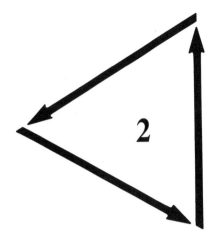

2

Organizing Your Hard Drive

CONCEPTS OF NETWORKING

Networking is the most efficient way to maximize a company's investment in personal computers. In addition to the ability to share files and peripherals, networking provides further advantages. For example, trustee rights can be applied to optimize security, and better control of how data is organized and maintained can be achieved.

The principal hardware components of a network consist of a file server, terminals, interface cards and cables. The file server is the brain or center of activity. It contains all of the information to be shared on the network. The terminals are nodes that receive and send information to and from the file server through cables by means of special interface cards placed in the terminals and the file server. Printers connected to the network and are shared by the entire network through a process called "spooling."

In addition to hardware, a network requires software to direct the flow of information between the various hardware and software components. Networking software also controls all the functions needed to coordinate network operation. One reason for Novell's popularity is that it is an open system; that is, it can be used with almost any network interface card in any

IBM or IBM compatible computer. Novell is also committed to bridging the "multiple environment" problem faced by many companies, in that it supports gateways to Apple Macintosh and VAX/VMS systems.

During the installation process of Novell the Network Operating System is customized. Novell is given specific information regarding the network environment. The installation of Novell is generally handled by the hardware vendor or a technically knowledgeable systems manager and is largely hardware dependent. This book will not deal with the installation process. For further information on the details of installation, refer to your Novell manual. However, certain information regarding the intended use of the network, particularly with consideration to users and software, must be provided to the person who is installing Novell. This input will determine how the hard drive will be organized.

WHAT WE MEAN BY ORGANIZING THE HARD DRIVE

To realize the full benefits of a network the file server must have a hard disk drive large enough to accommodate many users and software packages. Anything containing a great deal of information must be organized, otherwise chaos ensues. A hard drive is organized by using partitions and directories.

What Are Partitions?

The process of partitioning is the process of dividing the hard drive into manageable segments (called partitions or volumes) for use. For example a 330 megabyte hard drive might be divided into three sections, each one containing 110 megabytes.

What Are Directories?

The partitions can be further divided into directories. For example, partition number one might have a directory for WordPerfect, another one for user Susan and another one for letters.

HOW TO ORGANIZE PARTITIONS AND DIRECTORIES

You must weigh many factors when partitioning the file server hard drive. Always remember: you are working with totally raw storage space. You are the architect in charge of its design and layout.

First, how much raw space do you have to work with? Certainly a hard drive with a gigabyte would be partitioned differently than a hard drive with 330 megabytes. If the drive has less than 120 megabytes you might decide not to partition it at all. Novell NetWare limits each hard drive to 4 partitions. Each partition can contain a maximum of 255 megabytes. The number of directories allowed in each partition is determined during the installation process and depends upon the size of the partitions. Remember, partitioning is the first level of organization and the partition is going to be further subdivided.

Second, who will be using the drive space and what will they be using it for? How will your users be grouped and what type of files will they be writing to the disk? For example, would it be easier to organize the hard drive by user groups, i.e., in a retail organization you might want a partition for sales, another one for accounting. Will the sales group need more room than the accounting group? Another possibility is to partition by document group, i.e., in a law firm you might have a partition for litigation and another for corporate. Again, it is important to keep in mind that the size of your space or hard drive will, to some extent, determine the organization and size of your partitions. Remember, partition is the broadest level of division of your drive. It will be further subdivided.

Third, consider the type of data being created. For example, if you are working with extremely large databases, you must be sure the partitions are large enough to accommodate the files comfortably.

A fourth consideration, when setting up partitions, is trustee rights. Trustee rights control access to, and use of, files. Trustee rights are explained further in Chapter 3. For purposes of partitioning, remember that trustee rights start at the top of a partition and dribble down through all the partitions's groups and/or users to all directories and subdirectories in the partition. An example would be access to accounting information. If your accounting program is installed in partition number three and all users in this partition are in one group (accounting), then every person in this partition can have full rights to all of the information in this partition. If you spread your accounting program and data among two or more partitions, you must keep track of exactly where these files are in order to assign the proper rights to this group. By keeping group trustee rights in mind as you decide which programs to put in each partition, you will make life easier for yourself.

A fifth consideration concerns your method of backup. If you are working on a network, you should be using some sort of tape backup system. Various systems accommodate different sizes of storage devices. If your backup cartridge can only hold 120 megabytes of information, you might want to limit the size of your partitions to 120 megabytes. This way you can backup an entire partition at a time; and the backup process can be accomplished at night or unattended because it will not be necessary to insert a new cartridge when the first one is filled. This makes it possible to rotate your backup procedure in an orderly fashion, partition by partition, ie., partition one is backed up on Monday, partition two is backed up on Tuesday, etc. Backups will be discussed more fully in Chapter 10.

THE ABC COMPANY EXAMPLE

Having pointed out a number of considerations, we will give you an example of this planning process. The ABC Company is a small manufacturer of paper products. They have installed a small network, with a 330 megabyte hard drive in the file server. The network is to be used for its accounting, billing, word processing, some desktop publishing for advertising, and primarily is a very large database to contain information about customers, orders, inventory, delivery, suppliers, etc. This database also links to the accounting and billing programs.

The accounting and billing programs and data do not take up a great deal of space, but they contain many sensitive files. Very few people in the organization should have access to them. The simplest way to limit access to this information is to give accounting a separate partition. Only members of groups in that partition have complete rights. We can limit access from groups in other partitions by giving members of those groups limited accounting rights.

On the other hand, the ABC Company expects the database to take up more space on the hard drive. Although it is to contain detailed information about almost every aspect of the company, most of the information is not sensitive. Virtually every employee of the company is responsible for updating the database and needs to be able to retrieve information from it. Although the database is linked into the accounting and billing program, the programs can be set up so that the link is not automatic but will be effected only when so instructed by an appropriate end user. Consequently, it is not necessary for the database to be in the same partition as the accounting and billing programs because access across partitions is effected by the modular programming methods used to create the database program. Almost complete rights are allowed all members of the groups in this partition.

The third partition is also small and is devoted to word processing and desktop publishing. With the exception of the program files, users can have complete rights to all data in this partition.

With this criteria in mind concerning space and trustee rights, we can partition the hard drive as follows: partition one, which contains the word processing and desktop publishing files and data, is to be 82 megabytes; partition two, which contains the database program files and data is to be 165 megabytes; and partition three, which contains accounting and billing program files and data, is to be 83 megabytes.

During the installation process, the directories public, system, login, and mail are automatically placed in the first volume. The explanation of how these directories are used by the system can be found in Chapter 3.

Because ABC Company's backup tapes hold 120 megabytes, the company can back up partitions one and three onto one tape each. Partition two, however, must be backed up onto two tapes. Because it is best to backup the system at night, partition two can be backed up by directory over a period of two nights.

Figure 2-1 is a diagram of how our hard drive is going to look with our three partitions.

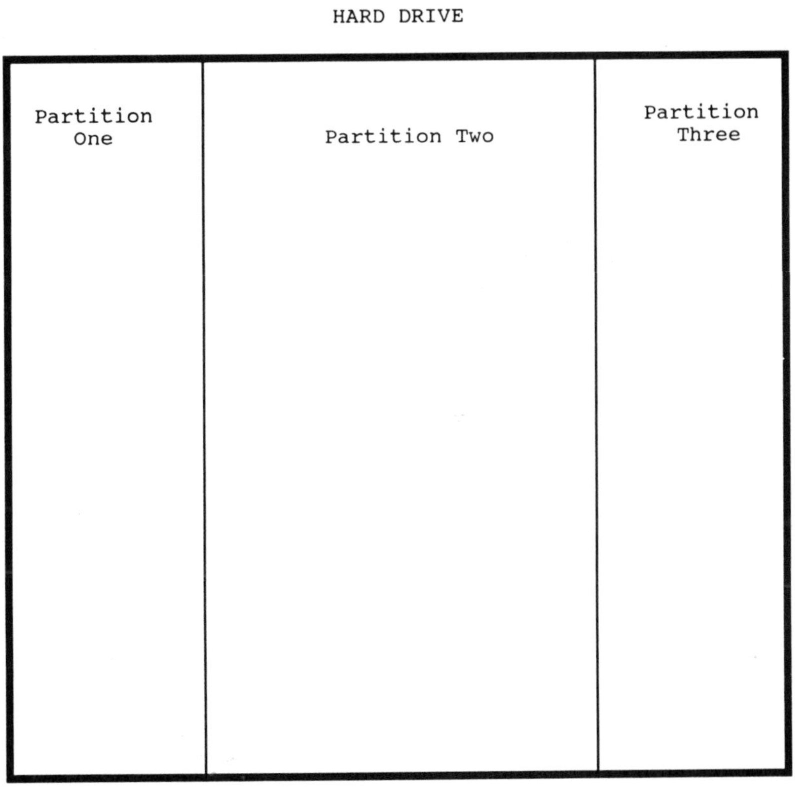

HARD DRIVE

Partition One	Partition Two	Partition Three

Fig. 2-1. Hard drive with three partitions

Partitions are given names by the user during the Novell installation process. So far we have determined that our partitions will accommodate wordprocessing in partition one (which was named SYS:); database in partition two (which was named SYS2:) and accounting in partition three (which was named SYS3:). (NOTE: The NetWare default for the first partition is SYS:, not SYS1:. This is fixed and cannot be changed.)

Now that we have our partitions organized, it is time to further subdivide our hard drive into directories. We use directories to organize data by user, programs, and type of information.

Directories can be created using the DOS command, Make Directory (MD), or they can be created in Novell by using the Filer menu utility which is described in detail at the end of this chapter.

ABC is using WordPerfect for word processing and limited desktop publishing applications. They also have additional soft fonts to further enhance their output. Because the users are secretaries whose work cannot be grouped by department or type of data, the best way to organize their directories is by user.

Each software program should have its own directory. Therefore, we set up a directory called WP for the WordPerfect program files. It is also a good idea to place the additional soft fonts in their own directory. That way they can be accessed by all programs capable of using them. ABC is using Bitstream Fonts, which is placed in a directory called FONTS.

There are six secretaries using the WordPerfect and Bitstream Fonts. Each secretary will have his/her own subdirectory as follows: Anne, Jane, George, Mary, Susan and John. In addition, Ellen, the accounting clerk, also needs a directory for WordPerfect. This is a total of seven user directories, each of which is identified by the user's name. Refer to Fig. 2-2.

For their database, ABC is using software customized for their needs. The program requires five directories: one for the database program files (called SYS2:DB); one for raw materials inventory and vendors (called SYS2:DB/MATERIAL); one for the complete client base (called SYS2:DB/DATA); one for sales made, i.e., orders placed (called SYS2:DB/SALES); and one for the tickler system (called SYS2:DB/TICKLER).

The accounting department requires four directories: one for the accounting program files (called SYS3:ACCT); one for accounts payable and accounts receivable (called SYS3:PAYDATA); one for payroll (called SYS3:GL); and a fourth directory for the information concerning sales orders (SYS3:ORDERS). This last directory is imported from sales into accounting. Figure 2-2 schematically shows how ABC Company's hard drive is divided by partition and directory.

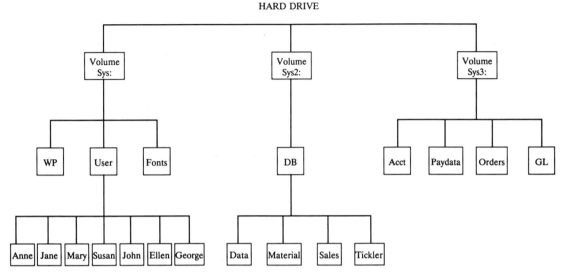

Fig. 2-2. Hard drive with partitions and directories

WHAT IS FILER AND HOW IS IT USED?

Filer is a Novell menu utility which helps you to monitor and control volume, directory and file information. The extent to which you can use Filer to make network changes or view information is limited by your trustee rights to perform particular tasks. To access Filer, at the DOS prompt type FILER Enter. The Filer main menu should appear on your screen (see Fig. 2-3). Unless you change the current directory (see Changing Current Directory on page 42), Filer provides information about

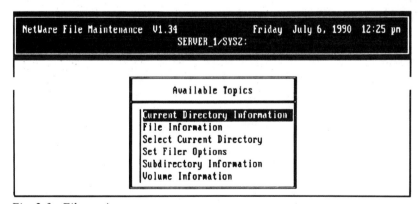

Fig. 2-3. Filer main menu

the directory in which you are currently working. This is called the current directory.

Filer and Volumes

Filer allows you to view information about the volume in which your current directory is located. You cannot make volume changes in Filer, only view information. In order to access Volume Information, you must be in the Filer Available Topics menu. Highlight Volume Information and press Enter. The following information is displayed:

- Server Name
- Volume Name
- Total Bytes
- Bytes Available
- Maximum Directory Entries
- Directory Entries Available

Most of these parameters were set during the installation process of Novell. They can only be changed by running the NETGEN segment of installation again.

Filer and Directories

You can also view directory information with Filer. If you have rights to do so, you can change a directory's maximum rights mask, add and delete trustees and change trustees' rights in the directory.

Changing Current Directory   Filer provides information about your current directory. You may need information on another directory, however. To change your directory path, highlight Select Current Directory and press Enter. The current directory path will be displayed. Use your Backspace key to delete the current directory path, then type in the new path.

Features in Filer that control directory access are found in the Current Directory Information screen. From your Available Topics menu highlight Current Directory Information and press Enter. The menu screen should now look like Fig. 2-4.

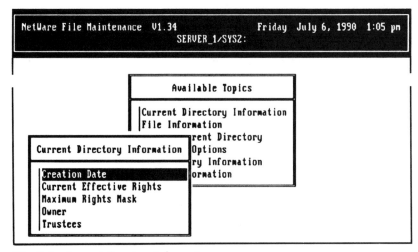

Fig. 2-4. Current directory information menu

When you highlight Creation Date and press Enter, you see the creation date of the current directory.

If you highlight Current Effective Rights and press Enter, your effective rights in the current directory are displayed. See Chapter 3 for a complete description of all trustee rights.

Changing the Maximum Rights Mask in Current Directory   The Maximum Rights Mask menu displays trustee rights for the current directory. If you possess effective Parental rights, you can add or delete rights to the directory while in this option. To access the Maximum Rights menu, select Current Directory Information and press Enter. Then highlight Maximum Rights Mask and press Enter. The Maximum Rights Mask list is shown in Fig. 2-5.

Adding and Deleting Rights in Current Directory   To add rights to the Maximum Rights Mask list, press Insert. The Other Rights list is displayed. Highlight the right you want to add and press Enter. To add more than one right, mark the rights you want to add with the Mark key (press F1 twice to confirm the Mark key for your computer) and Enter.

To delete rights from the Maximum Rights Mask list, highlight the right you want to delete and press Delete. When the Revoke Right box appears, highlight Yes and press Enter. To delete more than one right, mark the rights to be deleted with the Mark key (press F1 twice to verify the

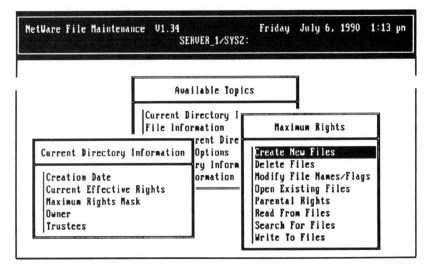

Fig. 2-5. Maximum rights mask list

Mark key for your computer) and press Delete. When the Revoke Right box appears, select Yes.

Viewing the Owner in Current Directory The Owner option displays the current directory owner. You can change the owner only if you have supervisor rights.

Adding and Deleting Trustees and Modifying Trustee Rights in Current Directory You cannot access the Trustees option unless you have Parental rights in the current or parent directory. The trustee option allows you to view and modify the trustee list in the current directory.

To view trustees and their rights, highlight Current Directory Information in the Available Topics menu and press Enter. When the Current Directory Information menu appears, highlight Trustees and press Enter. You are now in the Trustee Name/Trustee Type/Rights list, as shown in Fig. 2-6.

To add a trustee to the list in the Trustee Name/Trustee Type/Rights list, press Insert. The Others list appears, showing all of the users and groups on the network. Highlight the user or group you wish to add as a trustee and press Enter. To add more than one, mark the users or groups using your Mark key (press F1 twice to confirm the Mark key for your computer) and press Enter.

To delete trustees from the Trustee Name/Trustee Type/Rights menu, highlight the trustee and press Delete. When the Delete Trustee From Directory box appears, highlight Yes and press Enter. You have now

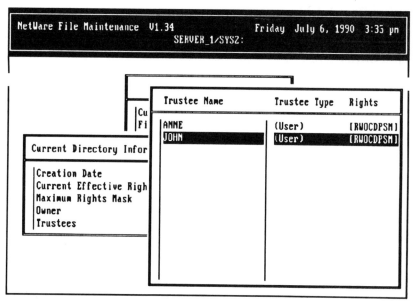

Fig. 2-6. Trustee name/trustee type/rights list

deleted this trustee from the trustee list of this directory. To delete several trustees, mark the trustees using your Mark key (press F1 twice to verify the Mark key for your computer) and press Delete.

To modify the rights of a trustee in the Trustee Name/Trustee Type/Rights list, highlight the trustee whose rights you wish to modify and press Enter. A list titled Trustee Rights appears, as seen in Fig. 2-7.

To add a trustee right from the Trustee Rights list, press Insert. The Other Rights list will appear. Highlight the right you wish to add and press Enter.

To add several rights, mark the rights you wish to add using your Mark key (press F1 twice to verify the Mark key for your computer) and press Enter.

To delete a trustee right from the Trustee Rights list, highlight the right you wish to delete and press Delete. A confirmation box titled Revoke Right will appear. Highlight Yes and press Enter. You have deleted a trustee right.

To delete several rights, mark the rights using your Mark key (press F1 twice to verify the Mark key for your computer) and press Delete.

Filer and Subdirectories

Using Filer's Subdirectory Information option you can: view subdirectory information; add, delete, and rename subdirectories; and, if you

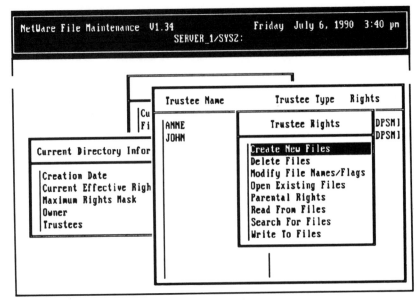

Fig. 2-7. List showing trustee rights for specific trustee

have the rights to do so, change the subdirectory's maximum rights mask, and add and delete trustees of the subdirectory.

To view a list of subdirectories of the current directory, highlight Subdirectory Information and press Enter. Figure 2-8 shows ABC's list of subdirectories of the current directory User.

Creating and Deleting Subdirectories   You can create a subdirectory in the current directory if you have Parental and Create rights. You can delete a subdirectory in the current directory if you have Parental and Delete rights.

To add a subdirectory, list the subdirectories of the current directory and press Insert. The New Subdirectory Name box will appear. Type in the new subdirectory name and press Enter.

To delete a subdirectory, list the subdirectories, highlight the subdirectory you want to delete and press Delete. To delete more than one subdirectory, use your Mark key to highlight each subdirectory you want to delete (verify the Mark key on your computer by pressing F1 twice.) The Delete Subdirectory Options menu will appear (see Fig. 2-9).

If you choose Delete Entire Subdirectory Structure the subdirectory, all files in that subdirectory and all subdirectories and files in the subdirectories under that level will be deleted. A confirmation box will appear asking you to confirm this choice.

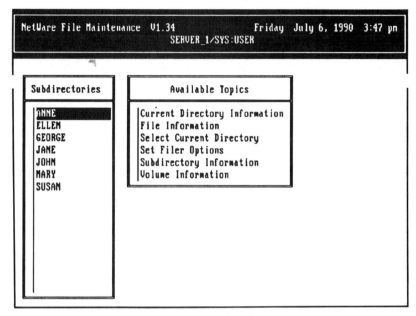

Fig. 2-8. Subdirectories of User directory listed in Filer

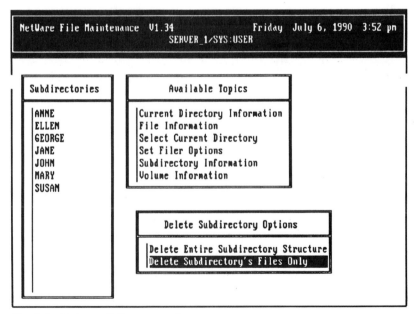

Fig. 2-9. Delete subdirectory options menu

If you choose Delete Subdirectory Files Only, only the files in the specified subdirectory will be deleted. The files in subdirectories under that level will not be affected. You will be asked to confirm this choice.

Where the subdirectory names follow a pattern, you can use the DOS wildcard (*) to delete groups of subdirectories. To do this, list the subdirectories and press F6. The Mark Pattern box will appear. Type the pattern of the subdirectories you want to delete. For example *.DOC will delete all subdirectories with a DOC extension. Then press Enter.

You can also exclude subdirectories that follow a pattern. If you press F8, the Unmark Pattern box will appear. Type the pattern for the subdirectory names you wish to exclude from the pattern delete feature. For example, Typing BOOK.* in the pattern box protects the subdirectory BOOK.DOC from deletion. Then press Enter. The Delete Subdirectory Options menu will appear. Select the appropriate option using the instructions given above.

CAUTION: DOS wildcards can be effective when deleting large numbers of subdirectories, but they should be used with caution and only by users who understand completely how they work. One mistake can cause a user to accidentally delete a great deal of data.

Renaming Subdirectories   You can rename a subdirectory only if you have Parental and Modify rights. To rename a subdirectory, list the subdirectories of your current directory, highlight the subdirectory you want to rename and press the Modify key (press F1 twice to verify the Modify key for your computer). The Edit Directory Name box is now on the screen. See Fig. 2-10.

Use the Backspace key to delete the old subdirectory name, then type in a new one and press Enter.

You can use the DOS wildcard (*) to rename groups of subdirectories where the names follow a pattern. See the section entitled Creating and Deleting Subdirectories in this chapter for information and a caution on using Mark Pattern and Unmark Pattern.

After you have marked and unmarked the appropriate subdirectories press the Modify key (press F1 twice to verify the Modify key for your computer). The Original Name Pattern box will appear. Type the original name pattern and press Enter. The Rename Pattern box appears. Type in the new subdirectory pattern and press Enter.

Creation Date and Time for Subdirectories   To view a subdirectory's creation date and time, list the subdirectories of your current directory, highlight the subdirectory you wish to view and press Enter. The

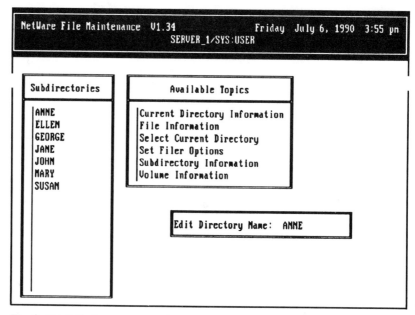

Fig. 2-10. Edit directory name box

Subdirectory Information list will appear. Highlight Creation Date and press Enter.

Changing the Maximum Rights Mask of Subdirectories You must have Parental rights to change the maximum rights mask in a subdirectory.

To view the current subdirectory's maximum rights mask, list the subdirectories. Next, highlight the subdirectory you wish to view and press Enter. When the Subdirectory Information menu appears, highlight Maximum Rights and press Enter. Figure 2-11 shows the Maximum Rights list.

To add rights while in the Maximum Rights list, press Insert. The Other Rights list will appear. Highlight the right you want to add and press Enter.

To add more than one right, mark the rights you want to add using the Mark key (press F1 twice to verify the Mark key on your computer) and press Enter.

To delete rights while in the Maximum Rights list, highlight the right you want to delete and press Delete. The Revoke Right box will appear asking you to confirm the deletion, highlight Yes and press Enter.

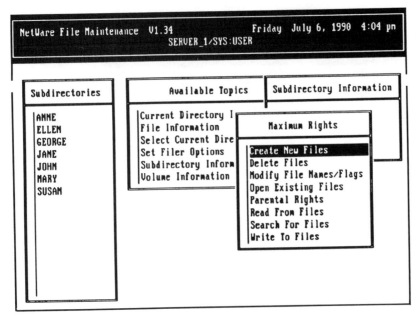

Fig. 2-11. Maximum rights list

To delete more than one right, mark the rights you want to delete using your Mark key (press F1 twice to verify the Mark key for your computer) and press Delete.

To modify rights for multiple subdirectories, list the subdirectories for your current directory. Use your Mark key (press F1 twice to verify the Mark key for your computer) to mark the directories in which you wish to modify rights and press Enter. The Multiple Subdirectory Operations menu will be displayed. Highlight Set Maximum Rights and press Enter. Then follow the above instruction for adding and deleting subdirectory rights.

Viewing Subdirectory Owner   To find who owns a subdirectory, list the subdirectories, highlight the appropriate subdirectory, and press Enter. When the Subdirectory Information menu appears, highlight Owner and press Enter. The name of the owner is now displayed on your screen.

Adding and Deleting Trustees and Modifying Trustee Rights of Subdirectories   You must have Parental rights to view or add trustees to a subdirectory. You must have Parental and Delete rights to delete trustees.

To view trustees and their rights, list subdirectories, highlight the appropriate subdirectory, and press Enter. The Subdirectory Information

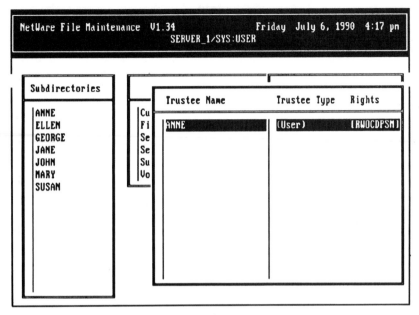

Fig. 2-12. Trustee name/trustee type/rights screen

menu appears; highlight Trustees, and press Enter. The Trustee Name/ Trustee Type/Rights list is now displayed, as shown in Fig. 2-12.

To add a trustee to the Trustee Name/Trustee Type/Rights list, press Insert. A list of groups and users on your current file server is displayed; highlight the user or group you are making a trustee, and press Enter. To add more than one trustee, use the Mark key (press F1 twice to verify the Mark key for your computer) to highlight each user or group you want to make a trustee and press Enter.

To delete a trustee from the Trustee Name/Trustee Type/Rights list, highlight the trustee you are deleting and press Delete. You will be asked to confirm the deletion. To delete more than one trustee, use the Mark key (press F1 twice to verify the Mark key for your computer) to highlight the trustees you want to delete, press Delete and then confirm the deletion.

To add trustee right to the Trustee Name/Trustee Type/Rights list, highlight the trustee's name and press Enter. You now have the Trustee Rights list (see Fig. 2-13). Now press Insert. The Other Rights list will appear. Highlight the right you are adding and press Enter. When you want to add more than one right, use your Mark key (press F1 twice to verify the Mark key for your computer) to mark the rights, then press Enter.

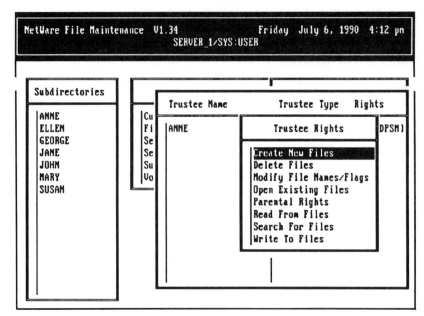

Fig. 2-13. Trustee rights list

To delete a user's trustee right from the Name/Trustee Type/Rights list, highlight the trustee's name and press Enter. The Trustee Rights list will appear. Highlight the right to be deleted and press Delete. When the confirmation box opens, confirm the deletion.

To delete more than one right, mark the rights being deleted with the Mark key (press F1 twice to verify the Mark key for your computer) and press Delete. When the confirmation box opens, confirm the deletion.

File Information

Filer also provides you with the ability to work with files in directories and subdirectories. While in your Available Topics menu, highlight File Information and press Enter. You will see a list of the files in your current directory (See Fig. 2-14).

Deleting and Renaming Files and Groups of Files   To delete a file, list the files in your current directory, highlight the file you want to delete, and press Delete. When the confirmation box opens, highlight Yes and press Enter. This confirms and deletes the selected file. To delete a group of files, mark each file by highlighting it and pressing the Mark key (press F1 twice to confirm the Mark key for your computer). After you

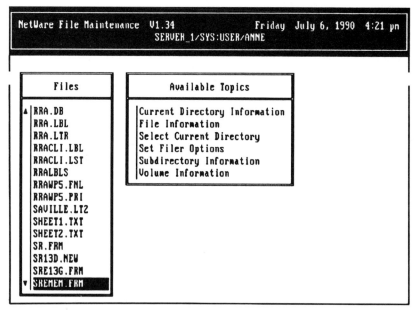

Fig. 2-14. List of files in current directory

have marked all the files you want to delete, press the Delete key. When the Delete All Marked Files confirmation box appears, highlight Yes and press Enter to complete the deletion.

You can use the DOS wildcard (*) to delete groups of files where the file names follow a pattern. To do this, list the files and press F6. The Mark Pattern box will appear. Type the pattern of the files you want to delete. For example *.DOC will delete all files with a DOC extension. Press Enter, then press Delete. You will be asked to confirm the deletion.

You can also exclude files that are marked with the pattern. If you press F8, the Unmark Pattern box will appear. Type the pattern for the file names you wish to exclude from the pattern delete feature. For example, LETTER.* will mean that the file LETTER.DOC will not be deleted. Press Enter, then press Delete and confirm the deletion.

To rename a file in the list, highlight the file and press the Modify key (press F1 twice to verify the Modify key for your computer). The Edit File Name screen will appear. Use the Backspace key to delete the old file name, then type in the new one and press Enter.

Using the Mark Pattern, F6, and Unmark Pattern, F8, boxes, you can rename a group of files using the DOS wildcard (*). For example, in a directory you can rename all of the files with a .DOC extension. After you have marked and unmarked the appropriate files press the Modify key (press F1 twice to verify the Modify key for your computer). The Original Name Pattern box appears. Type the original name pattern and press Enter. The Rename Pattern box now appears. Type in the new pattern and press Enter.

File Attributes

To view or modify a file's attributes, list the files in your current directory, highlight the desired file, and press Enter. (For further information on file attributes, see Chapter 3.) You now see the File Information menu, as shown in Fig. 2-15. Select Attributes from this menu to see a list of the file's attributes.

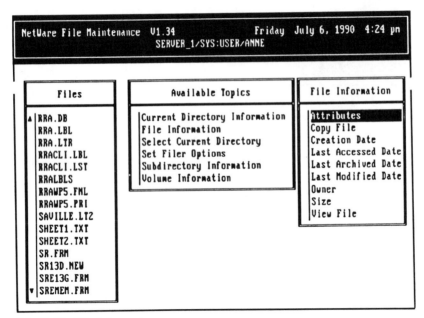

Fig. 2-15. File information menu

Adding File Attributes   To add a new attribute to the file selected from the File Attributes list, press the Insert key. A menu entitled Other File Attributes now lists all of the attributes not already granted to the file. Highlight the attribute you wish to add and press Enter. To add more than one attribute to a file, highlight each attribute to be added and mark it (press F1 twice to confirm the Mark key for your computer). Then press the Enter key.

You can add attributes to more than one file at a time. Highlight and mark each file (press F1 twice to confirm the Mark key for your computer).

Press Enter to see the Multiple File Operation menu. Highlight Set Attributes and press Enter. You now have a list of file attributes on the screen. To add an attribute to the list, press Insert to see the Other File Attributes list. Highlight the attribute to be added to the group of files and press Enter. If you wish to add more than one attribute, highlight each and mark it (press F1 twice to confirm the Mark Key for your computer). Then press Enter.

Deleting File Attributes   To delete an attribute from the file while in the File Attributes list, highlight the attribute you want to delete and press the Delete key. A confirmation screen appears. Highlight Yes and press Enter to confirm the deletion.

To delete more than one attribute, mark each attribute you want to delete (press F1 twice to confirm the Mark key for your computer) and press Delete. A confirmation box entitled Remove All Marked File Attributes appears. Highlight Yes and press Enter.

To delete an attribute from more than one file at a time mark each file (press F1 twice to confirm the Mark key for your computer). Then press the Enter key. The Multiple File Operations menu appears. Place your highlight on Set Attributes and press Enter. A list of file attributes appears. Highlight the attribute you want to delete and press the Delete key.

To delete a group of attributes from a group of files, mark (press F1 twice to confirm the Mark key on your computer) each file from which you are deleting attributes and press Enter. Now mark all the attributes to be deleted and press Delete. The Remove All Marked File Attributes box appears. Highlight Yes and press Enter. Now press Escape to see the Set Marked Files To Specified Attributes box. Highlight Yes and press Enter.

If you are deleting attributes from a file or group of files which have both Hidden and System attributes, delete both. Either of these attributes causes a file to be hidden (i.e., they will not be seen in a list of files). Deleting only one of these attributes does not allow the file to be seen. You must delete both. File attributes are discussed in greater detail in chapter 3.

To Copy Files

To copy a file, first list the files in your current directory. Next, highlight the file to be copied, and press Enter. The File Information menu appears. Highlight Copy File, and press Enter. A screen entitled Destination Directory will appear. Type in the full path or the mapped drive letter you are copying the file to and press Enter. The file has now been copied into another directory or subdirectory. You cannot mark and copy a group of files using this utility.

File History

Filer also shows you the history of a file. List the files in your current directory, highlight the correct file and press enter. You can now view the following information about the file:

1. Select Creation Date to see the date the file was created.

2. Select Last Accessed Date to see the last date the file was accessed.

3. Select Last Archive Date to see when the file was last archived.

4. Select Last Modified Date to see when the file was last modified.

5. Select Owner to find out who owns the file.

6. Select Size to learn the number of bytes the file contains.

7. Select View File to view the file. If the file is in ASCII format, the text will appear on the screen. If it is not, you will see a combination of text and programming symbols. You can move around in the file by using your cursor arrow keys or the PgUp and PgDn keys. The View File option does not allow you to edit the file, only to see what it contains.

Set Filer Options

You use the Set Filer Options menu to temporarily change the defaults used both in file and subdirectory management. From your Available Topics menu, highlight the Set Filer Options and press Enter. The Filer Options Settings menu in Fig. 2-16 is now displayed.

Confirm Deletions Thus far, when you have deleted a file or group of files, you have been asked to confirm that deletion once and then the action was done. You can instruct Novell to ask for a confirmation for each file in a group before it is deleted. To do this, highlight Confirm Deletions and press Enter. You now see a confirmation box entitled Confirm Deletion Of Each File Individually. Highlight Yes and press Enter. When you exit Filer, you will be returned to the Novell default of No.

Confirm File Copies Novell version 2.1x does not allow you to copy groups of files. The Confirm File Copies menu is a leftover from previous versions and has no effect.

Confirm File Overwrites Normally, NetWare asks for confirmation when you attempt to copy a file into a directory that already has a file

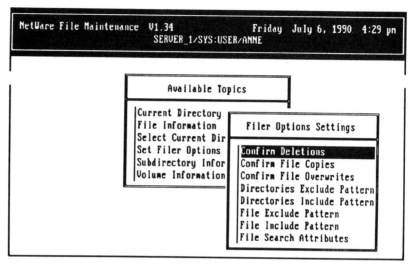

```
NetWare File Maintenance  V1.34              Friday  July 6, 1990  4:29 pm
                    SERVER_1/SYS:USER/ANNE


                    ┌──────────────────────────┐
                    │     Available Topics      │
                    ├──────────────────────────┤
                    │ Current Directory         │
                    │ File Information ┌─────────────────────────────┐
                    │ Select Current Dir        │ Filer Options Settings    │
                    │ Set Filer Options├─────────────────────────────┤
                    │ Subdirectory Infor│ Confirm Deletions          │
                    │ Volume Information│ Confirm File Copies         │
                    └───────────────────│ Confirm File Overwrites     │
                                        │ Directories Exclude Pattern │
                                        │ Directories Include Pattern │
                                        │ File Exclude Pattern        │
                                        │ File Include Pattern        │
                                        │ File Search Attributes      │
                                        └─────────────────────────────┘
```

Fig. 2-16. Filer options setting menu

with the same name. This action prevents files from being accidentally overwritten. You can instruct Novell not to prompt you for overwrites. Remember, if you do select this option, Novell will overwrite the old file with the new one. To allow unprompted overwrites, highlight Confirm File Overwrites, press Enter, and select No. The Novell default is Yes. When you exit the Filer menu utility, the default is restored.

Directories Exclude Pattern   You can use DOS wildcard (*) to exclude a group of directories or subdirectories when listing directories or subdirectories. First, highlight Directories Exclude Pattern and press Enter. The Exclude Directories Pattern list appears. Next, highlight the pattern you want to exclude and press Enter. If there are no entries, you can create one. Press Insert to activate the New Pattern box. Type in the new pattern and press Enter. Now when you list directories or subdirectories, only the ones not containing the selected pattern appear. For example, you have selected *DATA in the Directories Exclude Pattern. When you list the subdirectories in your current directory no subdirectories with DATA in its name will appear on the list.

To edit an entry in the Directories Exclude Pattern menu, highlight the pattern to be edited and press the Modify key (press F1 twice to verify the Modify key on your computer). The Edit Pattern box will appear. Change the pattern, and press Enter.

A pattern can be deleted from the Directories Exclude Pattern list. Highlight the entry you want to delete and, press Delete. When the confirmation box opens, highlight Yes and press Enter to delete the pattern.

Directories Include Pattern   You can also list directories and subdirectories to meet certain conditions. For example, if you want to list only subdirectories beginning with S, you would highlight Directories Include Pattern and press Enter. The list now displayed shows the DOS wildcard (*)—the default pattern that includes all directory patterns. To add a new pattern press Insert. The New Pattern entry box will appear. Type the pattern you want (S*) and press Enter. Now when you list directories or subdirectories, only those beginning with S will be included.

You can edit an entry in the Directories Include Pattern list by highlighting the pattern you want to edit and pressing Enter. When the Edit Pattern box appears, change the pattern and press Enter.

To delete an entry from the Directories Include Pattern, highlight the entry to be deleted and press Delete. When the confirmation box opens, highlight Yes and press Enter.

File Exclude Pattern   The File Exclude Pattern works in exactly the same manner as the Directory Exclude Pattern. Just highlight File Exclude Pattern and press Enter. Follow the previous instructions for the Directory Exclude Pattern.

File Include Pattern   The File Include Pattern works in exactly the same way as the Directory Exclude Pattern. Just highlight File Include Pattern and press Enter. Follow the instructions given for the Directory Include Pattern.

Adding and Deleting File Search Attributes   There are two file search attributes in Filer. They are Hidden and System. If they are not enabled, you cannot view system and hidden files. To add (or enable) them, do the following: highlight File Search Attributes and press Enter. Press Insert to display a list of Other Search Attributes. Highlight the attribute to be added and press Enter. Remember: you must enable both attributes to be able to see the file.

To delete a file search attribute, highlight the attribute to be deleted and press Delete. Highlight the Yes in the confirmation box and press Enter. To delete both file search attributes at once, mark them with your Mark key (press F1 twice to confirm the Mark key on your computer). Answer Yes to the Delete All Marked Search Attributes confirmation box. As with the other Filer options, when you exit Filer, the search attributes are all set back to their default setting.

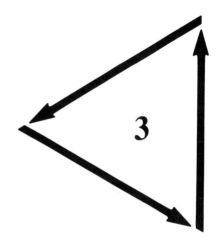

Groups and Users, Trustee Rights, and File Attributes

WHAT IS A USER?

A user is anyone who has access to a network. Users are added or deleted in Syscon (or added in Makeuser) and, only a supervisor or supervisor equivalent can add or delete a user or group of users on the network.

WHAT IS A GROUP?

A group is two or more users combined for the purpose of sharing trustee rights to directories. While groups are not essential, they certainly make it easier to manage a network. By grouping users according to access requirements, you eliminate the need to assign access levels to directories for each individual user. For example, ABC Company has a group called Accounting. Everyone in this group has complete trustee rights to all accounting directories. Other groups and users have very limited access to the accounting directories. Groups are created in Syscon, and group trustee rights can be assigned either in Syscon or Filer.

WHAT ARE TRUSTEE RIGHTS?

Trustee rights control user and group access to files and directories. There are eight possible trustee rights that you can assign to a user or group in a directory or subdirectory:

- Read from files
- Write to files
- Open existing files
- Create new files
- Delete files
- Parental rights
- Search for files
- Modify file name/flags

These rights are defined at the end of this chapter.

HOW ARE TRUSTEE RIGHTS ASSIGNED?

In order for an individual to access a directory or subdirectory, that individual must either be made a trustee of the directory or subdirectory or he must belong to a group that is a trustee of that directory or subdirectory. Users or groups can only be created in Syscon or Makeuser but can be made a trustee of a directory or subdirectory in either Syscon or Filer.

As we discussed in Chapter 2, each directory and subdirectory has a maximum rights mask that can be accessed and changed in Filer. This mask contains the *maximum* rights that can be assigned any user (other than a supervisor or supervisor equivalent) in a directory or subdirectory. If a right is deleted in the maximum rights mask, it cannot be assigned to any user, either through Syscon or Filer. If the maximum rights mask contains all rights, then these rights can be assigned to users or groups either through Syscon or Filer. To assign trustee rights to a user or a group in Syscon, a person must be a supervisor or supervisor equivalent. In order to add a right for a trustee to a directory or subdirectory in Filer, however, a user needs only Parental Rights in that directory or subdirectory. To delete a right for a trustee to a directory or subdirectory, the user must have Delete and Parental Rights in that directory or subdirectory (see Filer in Chapter 2).

WHEN TO USE SYSCON AND WHEN TO USE FILER

As discussed above once users or groups have been added to the network by the supervisor, he can use either Syscon or Filer to assign them trustee rights in a directory or subdirectory. It is usually more efficient to assign trustee rights to a user or group in several directories or subdirectories with Syscon. If you have created a new directory or subdirectory, it is more efficient to assign trustee rights by adding users or groups to the directory or subdirectory through Filer.

Adding and deleting trustee rights is explained completely in Chapter 2 under Filer. Adding and deleting trustee rights through Syscon will be explained fully later in this chapter.

WHAT ARE FILE ATTRIBUTES?

File attributes are rights which are assigned, either to individual files or all files in a directory or subdirectory. These rights can be assigned in Filer or through the Novell command line utility Flag. For information on how to set file attributes through Filer see chapter 2, Filer. This chapter covers assigning attributes through the Flag command.

There are ten attributes you can assign files in Novell:

- Execute Only
- Hidden File
- Indexed
- Modified Since Last Backup
- Read-Only
- Shareable
- System File
- Transactional
- Read-Write
- Non-Shareable

These attributes are defined at the end of this chapter.

TRUSTEE RIGHTS AND NETWORK SECURITY

Trustee and file rights are essential to network security. They control each user's access to every file and directory on the network. A complete understanding of how these rights apply to groups, users, and files is the key to a well organized and secure network.

ADDING AND DELETING USERS
USING SYSCON

In Chapter 2, we set up the directories ABC Company needs for its network. Now we will add our users and groups and define their trustee rights. There are two ways to add and delete users to the network: Syscon, a Novell Menu Utility; and Makeuser, a Command Line Utility. In the following example, we are using the Novell Menu Utility Syscon to add and delete users. For information on how to use Makeuser, see Makeuser at the end of this chapter.

1. Type SYSCON at the DOS prompt and press Enter. Figure 3-1 shows the Available to Topics menu.

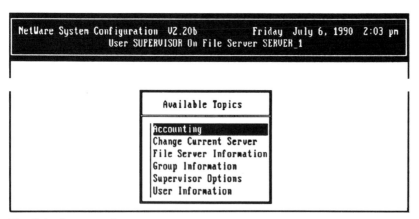

```
NetWare System Configuration  V2.20b          Friday  July 6, 1990  2:03 pm
                 User SUPERVISOR On File Server SERVER_1


                        ┌─────────────────────────┐
                        │     Available Topics     │
                        ├─────────────────────────┤
                        │ Accounting               │
                        │ Change Current Server    │
                        │ File Server Information   │
                        │ Group Information        │
                        │ Supervisor Options       │
                        │ User Information         │
                        └─────────────────────────┘
```

Fig. 3-1. Syscon main menu

2. Use the down arrow to highlight the User Information option and press Enter. The User Name box opens, as shown in Fig. 3-2.

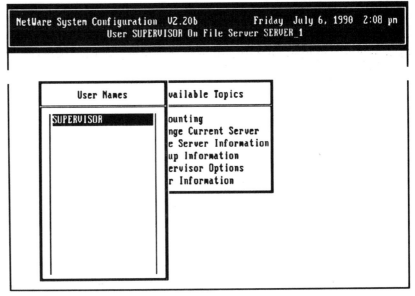

```
NetWare System Configuration  V2.20b          Friday  July 6, 1990  2:08 pm
                    User SUPERVISOR On File Server SERVER_1
```

User Names	vailable Topics
SUPERVISOR	ounting
	nge Current Server
	e Server Information
	up Information
	ervisor Options
	r Information

Fig. 3-2. User names menu

3. To add a user to the network press the Insert key. Type the name of the user you wish to add—in this case ANNE—at the User Name: prompt, and Enter (Fig. 3-3).

Anne's name now appears in the User Names list.

We continue adding the rest of ABC Company's users to the network by pressing Insert and typing each user's name at the User Name: prompt. We will add Jane, George, Mary, Susan, John, Ellen, Gus, and the owner of ABC Company, Bob. To exit Syscon and return to the DOS prompt, continue pressing Esc until you return to the Syscon Main Menu entitled Available Topics and press Esc once more. You will be asked to confirm this choice. Highlight Yes and press Enter.

When a user leaves ABC Company, you will need to remove him/her from the user list. Do the following to delete a user:

1. Type SYSCON Enter at the DOS prompt.

2. Highlight User Information and press Enter.

3. Highlight the name of the user to delete and press Delete. You will be asked to confirm the deletion. Highlight Yes and press Enter.

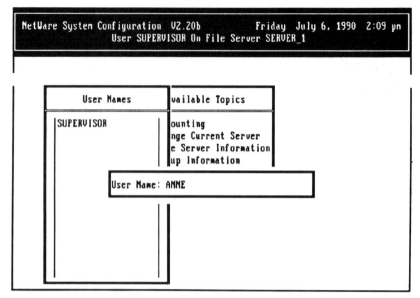

Fig. 3-3. Adding user Anne to the network

ADDING AND DELETING GROUPS USING SYSCON

As previously mentioned, when you have a number of users who will need the same trustee rights, it is more efficient to add them to the network and assign trustee rights by organizing them as a group. ABC Company needs three groups. Novell NetWare has already created a default group called Everyone. Therefore, we need to create two more groups: one for the accounting department, and another for the sales people. Gus (the accountant) and Bob (the owner of the company) both should have complete rights in the accounting group. They also need complete rights to all the information in the database program. Ellen (the accounts payable and receivable clerk) should have limited rights to accounting. Because she also imports the sales information from the database into accounting, she needs rights to the directory SYS2:DB/SALES. The sales people need rights to all of the data directories used by the database program but do not need to access accounting. Everyone should have rights to word processing, DOS, and the complete client list, which is in the directory SYS2:DB/DATA. Because the system has already created the group Everyone and includes all users, we do not have to do anything with that group. Our next step is to create the group called accounting and add our users. To accomplish this, do the following:

1. Type SYSCON and press Enter at the DOS prompt.

2. Highlight Group Information and press Enter.

3. Press the Insert key and type ACCOUNTING at the New Group Name: prompt. Press Enter and you now see that a group called Accounting has been added to the Group Names list.

4. In the Group Names list, highlight Accounting and press Enter.

5. Highlight Member List and press Enter.

6. Press Insert to add a member to the group. A screen entitled Not Group Members appears listing all users who are not currently members of the group. A single user is added by highlighting the user you want to add and pressing Enter. To add more than one user to the group (we will add Gus and Bob), use your Mark key (press F1 twice to verify the Mark key for your computer) to select each user you wish to add then press Enter. The names of those users who have been added to the group will now appear on the Group Members list.

To delete a member from the accounting group, follow these steps:

1. Type SYSCON and press Enter at the DOS prompt.

2. Highlight Group Information and press Enter.

3. Highlight Accounting and press Enter.

4. Highlight Member List and press Enter.

5. Highlight the member you wish to delete and press Enter.

6. When the confirmation box appears, highlight Yes and press Enter.

To delete more than one member from the Member List, use your Mark key to mark each member you want to delete (press F1 twice to verify the Mark key for your computer), press Delete, and confirm the deletion.

The Database group is created in the same way. Once you have created the group, add all the sales people as members of this group. Just follow the steps 1 through 6 above to add each user.

ASSIGNING TRUSTEE RIGHTS TO GROUPS

Now that we have created all of the groups that ABC Company will be using, we must assign trustee rights to each group.

Syscon allows a supervisor or supervisor equivalent to assign, add, or delete trustee rights for both groups and users. By following the instruction below, we are going to assign trustee rights to the members of the groups Everyone, Accounting, and Database.

1. Highlight the Group Information option on the Available Topics menu and press Enter.

2. In the Group Names list, highlight Everyone and press Enter.

3. You are now in the Group Information menu. Bring your highlight down to Trustee Directory Assignments and press Enter.

4. To add a directory in which to assign trustee rights, press Insert. A screen entitled Directory In Which Trustee Should Be Added will appear.

5. Type in the directory by identifying both the volume and the directory (e.g., SYS:WP) and press Enter.

Notice that the name of the directory appears on the left side of the screen and the trustee assignments appear on the right within brackets [R O S]. When you add a directory to the Trustee Directory Assignments, the system automatically assigns that directory the rights to read, open, and search. This means that all members of the group Everyone now have the rights to read, open and search for files in the WP directory. It is not considered advisable to give users all rights to program files because they would then be able to delete and/or modify them. The system has automatically given the group members all of the rights they need for WordPerfect.

Each member of the group Everyone (which includes all of the users of ABC Company) is also to be given default rights to the directories SYS:PUBLIC, SYS:SYSTEM, SYS:LOGIN, SYS:DOS, SYS:FONTS, and SYS2:DB by following steps 1 through 5 above. We also created a directory called DATA in SYS2:DB and one called user in SYS: with subdirectories under USER for each secretary and one for Ellen. Following steps 1 through 5 above, we will add the directories DATA and USER to the Trustee Directory Assignments list. This will, however, only give the members of the group the default trustee rights to those directories

[R O S] and to all of the subdirectories under them (remember that trustee rights filter down from a directory through its subdirectories unless specifically reassigned). Because we expect the secretaries and Ellen to create, edit, and delete documents in these directories, we need to assign to them the trustee rights to enable them to do so. We accomplish this as follows:

1. At the Trustee Directory Assignments screen, place your highlight on SYS:USERS and press Enter. The Trustee Rights Granted screen will appear and will list all of the trustee rights that are currently available to members of the group for the directory that is highlighted.

2. To add a trustee right, press Insert to get the Trustee Rights Not Granted screen to appear. The screen displays all of the trustee rights that have not been made available to members of the group.

3. Highlight the trustee right you wish to add and press Enter.

4. To add more than one right, use your Mark key (press F1 twice to verify the Mark key for your computer) to choose each right you wish to add and press Enter. The rights you selected now appear on the Trustee Rights Granted screen.

The following trustee rights are to be added to the directory SYS:USERS at ABC Company: Create New Files, Delete Files, Modify File Names/Flags and Write To Files. Press Esc and the Trustee Directory Assignments screen appears as shown in Fig. 3-4.

We next add the same trustee rights to the directory SYS2:DB/DATA. All of the necessary trustee rights for each member of the group Everyone have been assigned in each directory. By following the same procedure, we can now assign directory trustee rights to all of the directories in the groups Accounting and Database.

To delete a trustee right from the Trustee Directory Assignments screen, highlight the directory from which you want to delete the right and press Enter. The Trustee Rights Granted screen will appear. Highlight the trustee right you wish to delete, press the Delete key, and confirm. To delete more than one trustee right in the Trustee Rights Granted screen, use your Mark key (press F1 twice to verify the Mark key for your computer) to select the trustee rights you wish to delete, press Delete, and confirm.

To delete a directory from the Trustee Directory Assignments screen, place your highlight on the directory, press Delete, and confirm. To delete

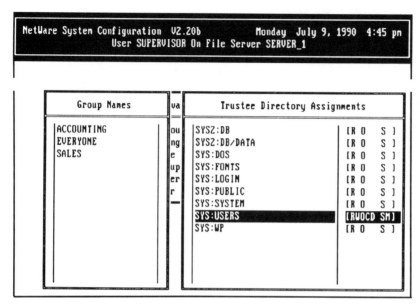

```
NetWare System Configuration  V2.20b           Monday  July 9, 1990  4:45 pm
                    User SUPERVISOR On File Server SERVER_1
```

Group Names	va	Trustee Directory Assignments	
ACCOUNTING	ou	SYS2:DB	[R O S]
EVERYONE	ng	SYS2:DB/DATA	[R O S]
SALES	e	SYS:DOS	[R O S]
	up	SYS:FONTS	[R O S]
	er	SYS:LOGIN	[R O S]
	r	SYS:PUBLIC	[R O S]
	—	SYS:SYSTEM	[R O S]
		SYS:USERS	[RWOCD SM]
		SYS:WP	[R O S]

Fig. 3-4. Trustee rights granted to directory SYS:USERS

more than one directory from the Trustee Directory Assignments screen, use your Mark key (press F1 twice to verify the Mark key for your computer) to select the directories you wish to delete. Press the Delete key and confirm.

ASSIGNING TRUSTEE RIGHTS TO USERS

All of the users at ABC Company have now been granted all of the trustee rights to every directory they need to access except Ellen. Ellen is not a member of either Database or Accounting because she does not need trustee rights to all of the directories in those groups. She does, however, need trustee rights to the directory SYS2:DB/SALES in the Database group and to the directories SYS3:ACCT and SYS3:ACCT/PAYDATA in the Accounting group. In order to give Ellen trustee rights to these directories, we could create a group especially for her; but because she would be the only member of the group, it makes more sense to assign the trustee rights to Ellen as a user. We do this using the following procedures in Syscon:

1. In the Available Topics menu, highlight User Information and press Enter. The User Names list will appear.

2. Place your highlight on ELLEN and press Enter. The User Information menu appears as shown in Fig. 3-5.

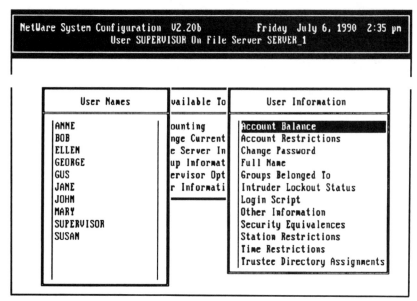

Fig. 3-5. User information screen for Ellen

3. In the User Information screen, highlight Trustee Directory Assignments and press Enter. The Trustee Directory Assignments screen appears as seen in Fig. 3-6.

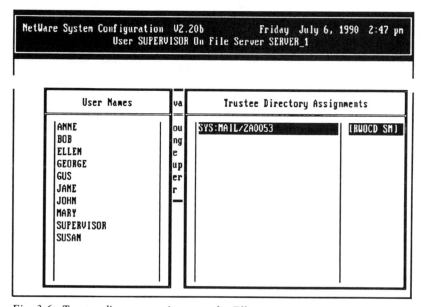

Fig. 3-6. Trustee directory assignments for Ellen

Notice that there is a directory to which rights have been granted already in existence. This is the SYS:MAIL directory. It has been added during the installation process with trustee rights to each user by the system.

4. While in the Trustee Directory Assignments screen, press Insert. A box should appear, entitled Directory in Which Trustee Should be Added. Type in the name of the directory you wish to add (for Ellen we type in SYS3:ACCT) and press Enter. The directory should now appear in the Trustee Directory Assignments screen and has been given [R O   S] rights by the system.

Following the above procedures, we can add the directories SYS2:DB/SALES and SYS3:ACCT/PAYDATA to the Trustee Directory Assignments for Ellen. She now has access to all three directories but will only have trustee rights to read, open, and search for files in those directories. In order to import sales information from the database to accounting and to maintain both accounts payable and accounts receivable, Ellen will need more trustee rights in both SYS2:DB/SALES and SYS3:ACCT/PAYDATA. To add those trustee rights, do the following:

1. To add a trustee right to a directory in the Trustee Directory Assignments screen, highlight the directory and press Enter. The Trustee Rights Granted screen appears and lists all of the trustee rights currently available in that directory.

2. In the Trustee Rights Granted screen, press Insert. The Trustee Rights Not Granted screen will appear. Highlight the trustee right you wish to add and press Enter. To add more than one right, use your Mark key (press F1 twice to verify the Mark key on your computer) and press Enter.

We mentioned earlier in this chapter that trustee rights assigned to a directory filter down through all of its subdirectories. Thus, when we gave Ellen read, open, and search rights to the directory SYS3:ACCT, we also gave her those rights in every ACCT subdirectory. These subdirectories include information Ellen does not need to know and should not be allowed to access. To deny her access to this information, it is necessary to delete those rights from these subdirectories. To do this, we have to add these subdirectories individually to Ellen's trustee directory assignments and then delete all rights granted by the system.

1. To delete a trustee right in the Trustee Rights Granted screen, highlight the right you want to delete and press Delete. The right will be deleted when confirmed.

2. To delete several rights simultaneously, use your Mark key (press F1 twice to verify the Mark key on your computer) to mark each right, press Delete, and confirm.

3. Press Esc. Ellen's new Trustee Directory Assignment screen appears (Fig. 3-7).

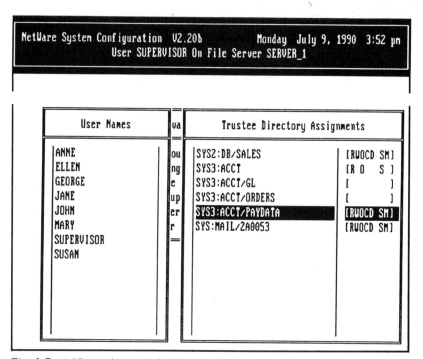

Fig. 3-7. *Additional trustee directory assignments granted to Ellen*

Explanation of Trustee Rights

Read Allows a trustee granted this right to read the contents of an existing, open file.

Write Allows a trustee granted this right to add to or change the contents of an existing, open file.

Open Allows a trustee granted this right to open existing files. If the trustee also has read and write rights he can then view, add to or change the contents of the files.

Create Allows a trustee granted this right to create a new file. Upon creation, the file is automatically opened. If the trustee has the parental right, Create allows the trustee to create subdirectories. (In NetWare Version 2.15 only, the parental right is unnecessary.) Even though a trustee with the create right can create a file, he cannot write to it unless he has write rights. Once the file is closed, unless the trustee has the open right he cannot reopen it.

Delete Allows a trustee granted this right to delete a file. If the trustee also has the parental right, it allows him to delete a subdirectory. (In NetWare version 2.15 only, the parental right is unnecessary.)

Parental Allows a trustee granted this right to assign trustee and directory rights to a directory and its subdirectories. The parental right also allows a trustee to change the Maximum Rights Mask in any directory in which the parental right has been granted. If a trustee also has create, modify and delete rights, then granting him the parental rights allows him to create, rename or delete the subdirectories of a directory.

Search Allows a trustee granted this right to list the files in a directory.

Modify file attributes Allows a trustee granted this right to change the attributes of files in the directory, rename directories and to rename files.

Definitions of File Attributes

Following is a list of file attributes. As indicated in the definitions, certain attributes can only be assigned or removed in the Filer utility. Others can be assigned or removed by using the command line utility Flag. An explanation on the use of the Flag command is found in Command Line Utilities following this section. For an explanation on how to use Filer, see Chapter 2.

Execute Only Files with .EXE and .COM extensions can be flagged Execute Only to prevent them from being copied off of the network. If you flag a file Execute Only there are two consequences you should keep in mind. Once you have flagged a file Execute Only you cannot undo the flag, you can only delete the file. Also, if your software has stored overlay files with its executable files, you might get error messages if the software tries to read the overlays in the execute file after loading. This attribute can only be assigned or removed in Filer.

Hidden File Files flagged as hidden do not appear when you run a DOS directory. In order for them to be seen, you must run Ndir. This attribute can only be assigned or removed in Filer.

Indexed If you flag a file as indexed, Novell indexes the File Allocation Table for faster access. Large data files should be indexed.

Modified Since Last Backup This attribute is assigned whenever a file has been modified. It is used by backup utilities to backup only those files that were modified since the last backup. The backup utilities normally remove this attribute when the file is backed up. If you need to assign or remove this attribute, you must use Filer.

Read-Only Files flagged Read-Only cannot be written to, renamed or deleted regardless of any trustee rights granted to the user.

Shareable Files flagged as shareable can be read by more than one user at a time.

System File Files that belong to the operating system are automatically flagged as system files and should not be changed. This attribute can only be assigned or removed in Filer.

Transactional Flags files to track transactions using NetWare Transaction Tracking. (This attribute is only available to users with Novell NetWare/SFT.)

Read-Write Files flagged with this attribute allow users to read, write to, rename or delete the file depending on their trustee rights. Read-Write is the default attribute when a file is created.

Non-shareable   Files flagged as Non-shareable can be accessed by only one user at a time. Non-shareable is the default attribute when a file is created.

COMMAND LINE UTILITIES
Flag

Syntax   FLAG [*path*] *filename*
FLAG [*path*] *filename* [option]

Purpose   Flag is used to change the attributes of a file. If you use the FLAG command by itself, the system will list the current flags on the file. The Command Line Utilities file flags are shown below:

Flag	Description
S	Shareable
NS	Non-Shareable
RO	Read-Only
RW	Read-Write
N	Normal (Flag a file Non-shareable and Read-Write)
T	Transactional
I	Indexed
SUB	Affects files in current directory and all subdirectories

NOT can be included before any of the flags listed above except Normal and Subdirectory.

Example   FLAG SYS:WP/*.PRN
This gives you a listing of all the .PRN files in the SYS:WP directory with the current flags.

Example   FLAG SYS:WP/*.PRN S RO

This changes all of the flags for the .PRN files in the SYS:WP directory to shareable, read-only.

Grant

Syntax   GRANT [*option*] FOR [*path*] TO [*user*] | [*group*]

Purpose   Use this Command Line Utility to grant trustee rights to users or groups. You can grant trustee rights to only one user or group for each Grant command. You may, however, grant up to all eight of the trustee rights for each Grant command. Before you can grant rights to users or groups, they must exist on the network. The Grant command adds a user or a group to the trustee list of a directory. The rights you can grant are as follows (complete explanations of the first eight are found in the section headed Explanation of Trustee Rights in this chapter):

> Read
> Write
> Open
> Create
> Delete
> Parental
> Search
> Modify
> No Rights—Revokes all rights
> All—Grants all eight trustee rights

You may also specify Only or All But before any of the first eight trustee rights listed above. By specifying Only, you grant only the specified right. If you specify All But, you grant all rights except the specified right.

Example   GRANT ALL FOR SYS:WP TO EVERYONE

This example grants all eight trustee rights in the directory SYS:WP to all of the members of the group Everyone.

Example   GRANT R W O C M S FOR SYS:WP TO ELLEN

This example grants the trustee rights read, write, open, create, modify, and search in the directory SYS:WP for user Ellen.

Makeuser

Syntax   MAKEUSER *usrfilename*

Purpose   Makeuser allows you to create or delete many users simultaneously. In order to use Makeuser as a command line utility, you must first create a USR file using the Novell Makeuser menu utility. (See Chapter 1 for details on the Makeuser menu utility.)

To use the Makeuser command line utility, you must be in the directory containing the USR files. It is therefore, a good idea to make a separate directory for all USR files.

Once you have created your USR file, simply type Makeuser and the name of the USR file at the DOS prompt. Novell will prompt you that your user has now been created.

It is important to remember that the system defaults in Syscon do not apply to users created with Makeuser. It is necessary to specify trustee rights assign users to groups, set accounting balances, and specify login and password restrictions through the use of the Makeuser keywords.

Remove

Syntax   REMOVE [user] | [group] [path]

Purpose   The Remove command will remove a user or a group from the trustee list of a directory.

Example   REMOVE ELLEN SYS2:DB/SALES

This removes the user Ellen from the trustee list of the directory SYS2:DB/SALES.

Revoke

Syntax   REVOKE [option] FOR [path] FROM [user] | [group]

Purpose   This command can Revoke up to all eight of the trustee rights a group or user can be granted in a directory. You can name as many trustee rights in this command as you wish, but you can only Revoke the rights for one user or group in any one Revoke command. If you wish to Revoke all eight trustee rights, you can replace the list of individual rights with the word ALL.

Example   REVOKE ALL FOR SYS2:DB/SALES FROM ELLEN

This example revokes all trustee rights in the directory SYS2:DB/SALES from Ellen.

Example   REVOKE D P FOR SYS3:ACCT/GL FROM GUS

This line revokes the trustee rights delete and parental from Gus in the directory SYS3:ACCT/GL.

SYSTEM, PUBLIC, LOGIN, AND MAIL

The directories SYS:SYSTEM, SYS:PUBLIC, and SYS:LOGIN are created by Novell during the installation process. These directories contain the NetWare system files, and their trustee rights should be limited to [R O S]. The directory SYS:MAIL is used by the system for E-Mail and the system itself will create a Trustee Directory Assignment for each user in Syscon and will assign rights to SYS:MAIL.

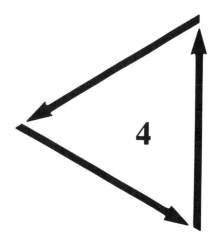

Login Scripts

LOGIN scripts are used to customize the network for each user. Their primary purpose is to create and modify drive and search maps, but they can also be used to create daily messages, customize the DOS environment, and to bring users to menus when they log on to the network with their unique user names. The system is then able to direct the user to the login script attached to that name and to execute all commands contained in that login script. In this way, the system is able to customize different environments for different users.

WHAT WE MEAN BY MAPPED DRIVES

To understand the function of login scripts, it is first necessary to understand how mapped and search drives work and why they are necessary in a network.

In Chapter 2, we discussed hard drive organization and the reasons hard drives are subdivided into directories. When you install a software package, you create a new directory for it off the root directory. All the files for that program are then copied/installed in that new directory. Each software program is, in the same way, installed in its own directory. Other directories can be created to contain the work files of a group of users (e.g., sales), individual users (e.g., John), or a class of documents (e.g., contracts). Keeping track of all these directories, however, can be very confusing. For this reason, Novell has made it possible to label or map directories to their own logical drives. These mapped directories are called logical drives. For example, the program WordPerfect 5.0 might be installed in a directory called F:\WP. To simplify locating this program, the directory can be mapped to a logical drive called S:. This logical drive is created using the Map command, either from the command line or in a login script. Once this is accomplished, the user can access WordPerfect simply by typing S: rather than by searching through all the directories and subdirectories to find the one containing WordPerfect.

Each letter of the alphabet can be used only once in a single login script. If they have been remapped using Novell's Menu utility (discussed in Chapter 6), Map command line feature (discussed in Chapter 1), or the Session menu utility (discussed in this chapter), it is possible to use letters over again. The syntax for mapping drives is as follows:

MAP *n:=volume:*[*directory*]

where *n* is a letter.

Remember: You must have created a directory before you can map it.

For additional information on mapping drives, see "MAP" in the "Login Script Commands" at the end of this chapter.

WHAT WE MEAN BY SEARCH DRIVES

Search drives allow the user to execute a program from anywhere in the network. For example, most programs are installed in their own directory, but the files created while using a program (e.g., a letter created with WordPerfect) should be installed in other directories. While Word-Perfect might be mapped to drive S:, the document files created by WordPerfect should be placed in other directories such as a user directory (John) or a document-type directory (letters).

When the program is executed, it is desirable to be able to execute it from the directory where the files are to be placed, so that the user does not have to change directories once he is in the program. To do this, it is necessary for the network to locate the execute file in order to run the program in a directory other than the one in which it is installed. This is done through the use of search drives. (Search drives in Novell are analogous to the path command in DOS.) The syntax for specifying a search drive is:

MAP Sn:=volume:[directory]

where n is a number.

The current drive maps for all directories on a workstation can be displayed by typing the command MAP at the DOS prompt.

To illustrate, let us continue with our WordPerfect analogy. John, a secretary at ABC Company, would like to create a document in WordPerfect and place it in his user directory. The best way to do this is to access his user directory (preferably through a menu set up by his supervisor) and to execute WordPerfect from within his directory. To do this, the system must be able to locate the WordPerfect execute file to run it in a directory other than F:WP. If a search drive has been set up in either the System Login Script or John's login script, Novell instructs the system to find the WordPerfect execute command and execute it in John's directory. If there is no search drive in either the System Login Script or John's login script, the system only searches John's directory for the WordPerfect execute file and then displays the message, "bad command or file name", because John's directory does not contain WordPerfect's execute file.

LOGIN SCRIPTS AND MESSAGES

Login scripts are also a convenient way to present messages to a user when he accesses the network. The messages can be customized by user or group or they can be system-wide. For example, Novell can be instructed to issue a message to a user to check his mail. This can be set up in such a way that the message will only appear if the user actually has mail, or Novell can be instructed to issue a different message for every day of the week.

Message commands can be either conditional or absolute. Condition messages only appear when one or more variable conditions are met. Absolute messages appear every time the user logs onto the network. In addition, users can change their own message or messages by modifying their own login scripts. Only the supervisor or supervisor equivalent can change the system message or messages by modifying the system login script. All of Novell's login script commands are listed and explained at the end of this chapter.

LOGIN SCRIPTS WITH MORE THAN ONE
FILE SERVER

If your network has more than one file server, it is advisable to designate a default server through either the System Login Script or individual User Login Script. Otherwise Novell determines which server the user is routed to when logging into the system. For the syntax to attach a file server in a Login Script, see "ATTACH" in the "Login Script Commands" at the end of this chapter.

Except for supervisory reasons, such as network backups, it is not advisable to attach to several file servers in a Login Script. This can be handled more efficiently through the Menu Utility, Session, or the Attach command line utility. See Chapter 6 for further information on Novell's Menu Utility. See Chapter 1 for further information on Session and command line utilities.

SYSTEM AND USER LOGIN SCRIPTS

Novell lets you use two levels of login scripts. One is the System Login Script; it affects all users as they log on the system. The other is the individual login script; it affects only the person using the login name associated with that script.

System Login Scripts can be written, modified, and accessed only by the network supervisor or supervisor equivalents through Novell's Syscon utility. System Login Scripts are accessed by selecting Supervisor Options in the Available Topics menu.

Each individual login script, on the other hand, can be accessed and modified by its own user. To do this, select User Information in the Syscon Available Topics menu. This activates the User Names list. Highlight your name and press Enter. A new User Information menu appears. Highlight Login Script and press Enter.

DIFFERENCES BETWEEN SYSTEM AND USER LOGIN SCRIPTS

Determining what information should be put in the system login script and what information should be put in user login scripts can be difficult. In general, the following rules apply:

1. Your System Login Script must contain search drives for Public, DOS, and Comspec volumes.

2. If you have multiple volumes, you should map a drive for each one in your System Login Script.

3. Your System Login Script should contain search drives to any software that is going to be used system-wide.

User Login Scripts contain information and commands specific to that user. In order for John to operate WordPerfect in his directory, his directory should be mapped in his user login script. This way his menu can be programmed to take him directly into his own directory, or he can access his own directory in DOS just by typing his mapped drive letter.

The customization of a user's login script can be determined by the user's job responsibilities. For example, let's discuss ABC's accounting program. Only two of the employees need to access anything other than Accounts Payable and Accounts Receivable. Because their software was custom written, it has been organized so that these Accounts Payable and Accounts Receivable files are in one directory. The files containing payroll, general ledger, balance sheets, etc., are in another directory. Therefore, the User Login Script for Ellen, an accounts payable clerk, maps her to the directory containing the Accounts Payable and Accounts Receivable files. Gus is the accountant for ABC Company, and his login script maps drives for both directories. Because each of these users access different program functions, their login scripts will take them to a different menu.

Occasionally, there is a conflict between the system login script and user login scripts. Where there is a conflict, the user login script overrides the system login scripts.

Creating the System Login Script

We will now create a System Login Script for ABC Company. We have considered all of the software that will be used by the employees of ABC and have decided that in addition to Public, DOS and Comspec (each of which must be in a search drive and able to be accessed by everyone), we will also include search drives for WordPerfect, the database program, and the accounting program. When we installed the database program, the program itself created a subdirectory for data that all users will access. We should, therefore, set up three mapped drives: one for volume SYS2:, one for volume SYS3:, and one for SYS2:DB/DATA. Because SYS: is the default volume, it is not necessary to map it.

The system supervisor or supervisor equivalent can create the System Login Script by following these steps:

1. Type SYSCON and press Enter at the DOS prompt. The Syscon Available Topics menu appears on your screen as shown in Fig. 4-1.

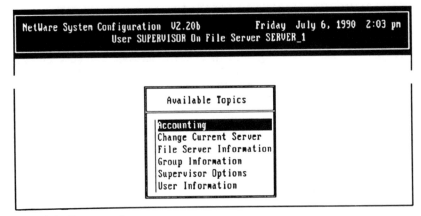

Fig. 4-1. Syscon main menu

2. Press the down arrow cursor key to highlight Supervisor Options and press Enter. The Supervisor Option menu is now on your screen, as shown in Fig. 4-2.

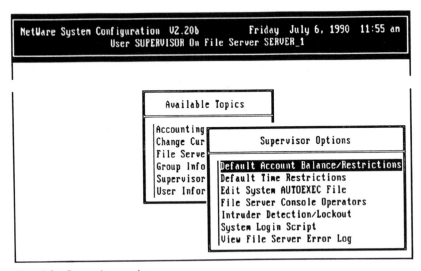

Fig. 4-2. Supervisor options menu

3. Highlight the option System Login Script and press Enter. You should now have an empty box on your screen labeled System Login Script. This screen is shown in Fig. 4-3.

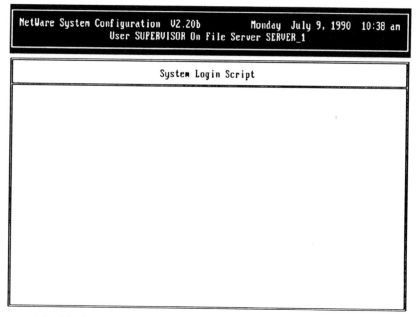

Fig. 4-3. Blank system login script

4. Type the text shown in Fig. 4-4 into the System Login Script box. Each line is completed by pressing Enter. Several of the Login Script command lines are longer than the display line length.

Let's review each command, line by line:

1. FIRE PHASERS 5 TIMES
   This command fires a phaser sound effect (like the phaser sound in Star Trek) five times when a user logs on to the system.

2. WRITE " \n \n Good %GREETING_TIME, %LOGIN_ NAME"
   This command does the following:
   • WRITE tells Novell to write this message to the screen.
   • " \n \n instructs Novell to skip two lines (Novell will skip one line for each \n). The first double quote mark, ", tells Novell to regard what follows as text; all text must be preceded and followed by a double quote mark. Any material designated as text will print as compared to commands that are not enclosed by double quotes and will not print.

```
NetWare System Configuration  V2.20b         Monday July 9, 1990  1:29 pm
                 User SUPERVISOR On File Server SERVER_1
```

```
                          System Login Script

FIRE PHASERS 5 TIMES
WRITE " \n \n Good %GREETING_TIME, %LOGIN_NAME"
IF DAY_OF_WEEK="Monday" THEN WRITE "\n \"It's Monday -- Have a Nice
Week\"\n\n"
IF DAY_OF_WEEK="Tuesday" THEN WRITE "\n \"TO ERR IS HUMAN, To Really Foul
Things Up Requires a Computer.\"\n\n"
IF MEMBER OF "Sales" AND DAY_OF_WEEK="Tuesday" THEN WRITE "\n \"DON'T
FORGET!!! TUESDAY SALES MEETING.\"\n\n"
IF DAY_OF_WEEK="Wednesday" THEN WRITE "\n \"Are We Having Fun Yet?\"\n\n"
IF DAY_OF_WEEK="Thursday" THEN WRITE "\n \"Don't Squander Time -- It It The
Stuff Life Is Made Of.\"\n\n"
IF DAY_OF_WEEK="Friday" THEN WRITE "\n \"TGIF!!\"\n\n"
IF DAY_OF_WEEK="Saturday" THEN WRITE "\n \"What Are You Doing Here On
Saturday?\"\n\n"
IF DAY_OF_WEEK="Sunday" THEN WRITE "\n \"Neither a Borrower Nor a Lender
Be.\"\n\n"

PAUSE
map display off
map g:=sys2:
map h:=sys3:
map i:=sys2:db/data
map s1:=sys:public
map s2:=sys:dos
comspec=s2:command.com
map s3:=sys:wp
map s4:=sys2:db
map s5:=sys3:acct
set prompt="$p$g"
```

Fig. 4-4. Final system login script

- Good %GREETING_TIME, %LOGIN_NAME"
  %GREETING_TIME indicates morning, afternoon, or evening
  and %LOGIN_NAME is the login name of the user. For example, if John logs in at 9:30 A.M., he will receive a message
  saying, "Good Morning, John."

3. IF DAY_OF_WEEK="Monday" THEN WRITE "\n \ "It's Monday—Have a Nice Week \"\n \n"

This command is conditional. If the day of the week is Monday, Novell is instructed to print this message upon login. In ABC's Login Script, each day of the week has its own message. IF . . . THEN conditions are explained further in the Login Script Commands at the end of this chapter. You will note that there is now a \ " immediately preceding and following the message. This extra " instructs Novell to surround the message with quotes.

4. IF MEMBER OF "Sales" AND DAY_OF_WEEK="Tuesday" THEN WRITE "\n\ "DON'T FORGET!!! TUESDAY SALES MEET-ING.\"\n\n"
   Two conditions must be true for this command to print the meeting message on the screen: The user must be a member of the group "Sales," and the day of the week must be Tuesday. If either of these conditions is not true, then this statement will not print. Groups are explained in Chapter 3.

5. PAUSE
   PAUSE tells Novell to pause at this point and instruct the user to strike any key to continue. DAY_OF_WEEK message will appear on the screen, and the execution of the login script will pause until the user strikes any key to instruct Novell continue the login script execution.

6. map display off
   Display Off commands Novell to turn the display off. This means that any instructions in the Login Script that follow this command will not be written to screen during the execution of the Login Script. The Map Display Off command instructs Novell to turn off the displaying of any mapping commands following the Map Display Off command.

7. map g:=sys2:
   ABC's hard drive has been divided into three partitions or volumes. They are SYS:, SYS2:, and SYS3:. This command maps SYS2: to drive G.

8. map h:=sys3:
   This command maps SYS3: to drive H.

9. map i:=sys2:db/data
   This command maps SYS2:DB/DATA to drive I.

10. map s1:=sys:public

    This command sets up a search path instructing Novell to read all execute and command files in SYS:PUBLIC even if the user is in another directory or volume.

11. map s2:=sys:dos

    This command sets up a search path instructing Novell to read all execute and command files in SYS2:DOS even if the user is in another directory or volume.

12. comspec=s2:command.com

    This command instructs Novell where to locate the DOS command.com file. It must be found by the system in order for Novell and other applications software to operate properly. If, upon exiting from an application software program, you receive a message asking you to insert a disk with command.com or system command interpreter, you should check to see if the Comspec command is in your System Login Script.

13. The remainder of the search paths in the System Login Script work the same way as steps 10 and 11 above. Note:
    • Numbers and letters (e.g., map g:; map h:; etc. or s1:; s2:;) can only be used once in a login script.
    • Your first search path (S1) should be the same path as the directory in which your menu is located. This applies whether you are using a system menu or individual user menus. If you are using individual user menus, then search path S1 will vary according to user.
    • A login script may use up to 26 logical drives (letters A–Z).
    • You can use up to 16 of these drives for search drives.
    • Command lines cannot exceed 150 characters.

14. set prompt=pg

    This is a DOS prompt command that instructs the system to display both drive and directory while working in DOS. Example: while working in WordPerfect, the DOS prompt will read as follows:

    F:\WP>

    assuming that WP has not been mapped to another drive.

ABC Company now has a System Login Script that, upon login, will greet each user, and deliver messages. It also allows access to DOS,

WordPerfect, the database program, and the accounting program from anywhere in the network. It is still necessary to fine-tune a login script for each user. This is our next step.

Creating User Login Scripts

We will now create a user login script for John, one of the secretaries at ABC Company. In addition to the search drives mapped for WordPerfect (map s3:=sys:wp) and the database program (map s4:=sys2:db) in the System Login Script, we need to map John to his own user directory for WordPerfect. Because Novell reads a User Login Script after reading the System Login Script, Novell will use the map created in the User Login Script if duplicate drivers are found. We can avoid this by using other unused letters of the alphabet to map our drives in the User Login Script.

We have previously created (in Chapter 2) a directory in SYS: called USER. Under the USER directory we created subdirectories for each user utilizing their first names. These subdirectories are to be used by each user for their word processing files. With our directories and subdirectories created, we are ready to set up John's User Login Script by following these steps:

1. Type SYSCON at the DOS prompt and press Enter. (See Fig. 4-1 to see the Available Topics menu.)

2. Press the down arrow key to highlight User Information and press Enter. This accesses the User Names list shown in Fig. 4-5.

3. Press the Down Arrow key to highlight John and press Enter. This accesses the User Information screen shown in Fig. 4-6.

4. Now highlight Login Script and press Enter. A box called Login Script Does Not Exist: appears. Press Enter again and a blank Login Script For User John screen appears (as seen in Fig. 4-7).

5. Type the following to create John's User Login Script:

```
map display off
map j:=sys:user/John
exit "menu main1"
```

Your screen should now look like Fig. 4-8.

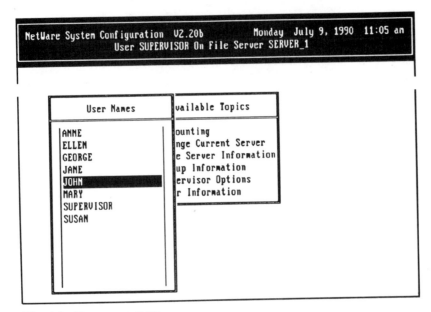

Fig. 4-5. User names menu

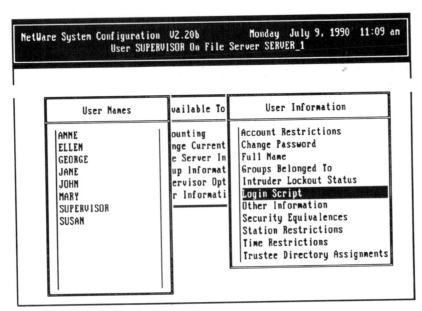

Fig. 4-6. John's user information menu

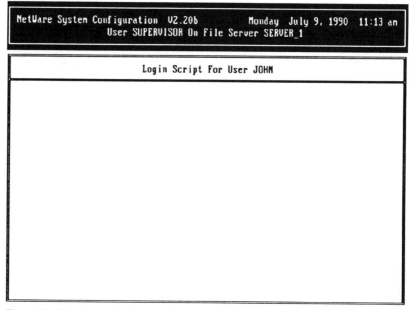

Fig. 4-7. Blank user login script for John

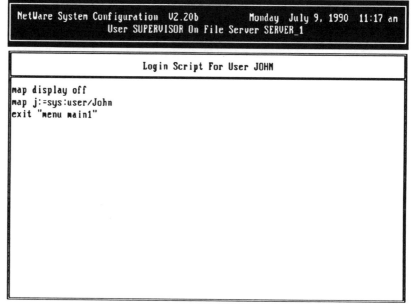

Fig. 4-8. John's finished user login script

Now let's review the commands we just entered.

1. map display off
   Just as it does in the system login script, map display off instructs Novell not to display the following mapping commands as the login script is executed.

2. map j:=sys:user/John
   This command maps the volume sys:, the directory user, and the subdirectory John to drive J:.

3. exit "menu main1"
   This command directs Novell to exit the login script and execute the Novell menu that has been written for the secretarial staff and has been named main1. Other menus have been written to accommodate other departments. For detailed information concerning Novell menu screens, see Chapter 6. For further information on the Exit command, see "Login Script Commands" at the end of this chapter.

Copying Login Scripts

Everyone in the secretarial department has similar logon requirements. Therefore, we can simply copy John's login script and edit the first map entry.

To copy John's user login script to Mary, follow these steps:

1. Type SYSCON Enter at the DOS prompt. You should now be in the Available Topics list.

2. Highlight User Information and press Enter. You should now be in the User Names list.

3. Highlight Mary and press Enter. You should now be in the User Information menu.

4. Highlight Login Script and hit Enter. You now have the screen shown in Fig. 4-9.

5. Where the menu says Read Login Script From User: backspace to delete Mary, type in the name John, then press Enter.

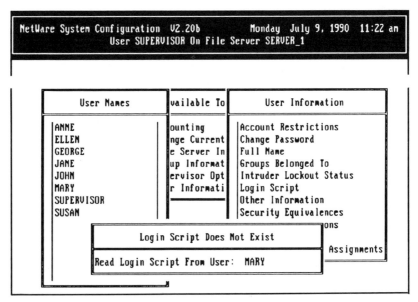

```
NetWare System Configuration  V2.20b          Monday July 9, 1990  11:22 am
                        User SUPERVISOR On File Server SERVER_1
```

User Names	vailable To	User Information
ANNE	ounting	Account Restrictions
ELLEN	nge Current	Change Password
GEORGE	e Server In	Full Name
JANE	up Informat	Groups Belonged To
JOHN	ervisor Opt	Intruder Lockout Status
MARY	r Informati	Login Script
SUPERVISOR		Other Information
SUSAN		Security Equivalences

```
                        Login Script Does Not Exist

              Read Login Script From User:   MARY
```

Fig. 4-9. Screen to copy login scripts to other users

6. John's Login Script has now been copied to user Mary. We only need to change the second line that now reads:

```
map j:=sys:user/John
```

This should be changed to read:

```
map j:=sys:user/Mary
```

Mary's Login Script now reads:

```
map display off
map j:=sys:user/Mary
exit "menu main1"
```

We will now create a user login script for Ellen, the accounts payable clerk at ABC Company. Ellen needs access to different information and programs than John.

When we installed the accounting program, it set up several directories. One of them contains both accounts payable and accounts receivable data. This directory is called PAYDATA. Ellen is also expected to help out the secretarial department if their workload becomes too heavy. Therefore, she has a subdirectory under the directory USER called Ellen. Because

Ellen's responsibilities have little in common with those of John or Mary, we are creating her user login script from scratch. We use the following steps:

1. Type SYSCON Enter at the DOS prompt to view the Available Topics menu.

2. Highlight User Information and press Enter. You are in the User Names list.

3. Highlight Ellen and press Enter. You are now in the User Information menu.

4. Highlight Login Script and press Enter. You now have the Login Script Does Not Exist box as seen in Fig. 4-10.

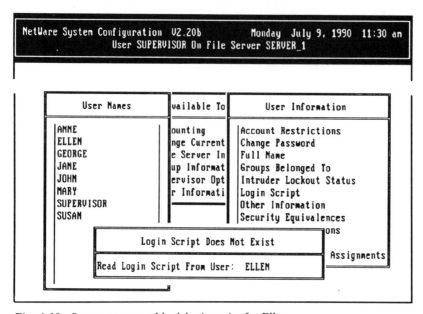

Fig. 4-10.   Screen to access blank login script for Ellen

5. Press Enter again. A blank Login Script is now on the screen. Type in the following:

```
IF LOGIN_NAME="Ellen" AND DAY_OF_WEEK="Friday"
THEN   WRITE"\n\"Today is Friday--Run Reports.\"\n\n"
map display off
map j:=sys:user/Ellen
```

```
map k:=sys3:paydata
exit "menu main2"
```

There are some additions to (as well as some differences between) Ellen's user login script and those of John and Mary. We have mapped SYS3:PAYDATA to drive K:. Because Ellen always forgets to run the weekly accounts payable and accounts receivable reports, we also included a reminder in her individual login script on Friday. This reminder does not affect the messages included in the System Login Script.

Notice that we have also reused drive J: which we have mapped to SYS:USER/Ellen. Because these are individual login scripts, it is possible for us to reuse mapped drives for each user without affecting other user's Login Scripts. The login script concludes by exiting to a different menu called Main2.

CREATING, DELETING, AND EDITING MAPPED DRIVES IN SESSION

Session, a Novell menu utility, can be used to temporarily map a drive or search drive for a particular workstation. Let's assume that John is going to be working all day on a report. This report is going to be put in a directory called TEMP, which he needs to access only for the one day it takes to generate the report. Rather than edit John's user login script, it makes more sense to map the TEMP directory to a temporary drive. To accomplish this, go to the DOS prompt and do the following:

1. Type SESSION and press Enter. The Session Manager Available Topics menu is now on the screen, as seen in Fig. 4-11.

2. Press the Down Arrow key to highlight Drive Mappings and press Enter.

3. In the Drive Mappings menu, press the Insert key on your keyboard. A small menu now superimposes itself on the Drive Mappings menu and says "Drive:" followed by the first available drive name. You have two choices here:
   • You can accept the default drive by pressing Enter.
   • You can use another drive letter. Just type in the letter of the drive you want and press Enter.

4. A screen superimposes the Drive Mappings menu asking you to Select Directory. You are ready to identify your mapped drive.

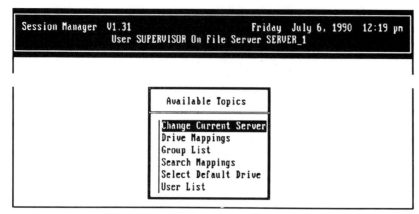

Fig. 4-11. Session main menu

Because Novell has already asked you for the name of your mapped drive, it is not necessary to enter it. It is, however, necessary in Session to identify the server, the volume, and the directory, when you map a drive. Enter the following:

SERVER_1/SYS:TEMP

5. If you do not know what server, volume, and/or directory name you want to map, press the Insert key:
   • A list of servers appears on a screen called File Servers/Local Drives. Highlight the one you want and press Enter.
   • Next, a list of volumes appears on a screen called Volumes. Highlight the one you want to select and press Enter.
   • Next, a list of directories appears on the Network Directories screen. Highlight the directory you want and press Enter.

6. Your selections are now reflected on the Select Directory screen. Press Esc to leave the directory listings. Now press Enter to accept the temporary drive mapping.

   Now, when John exits his menu and types the name of the mapped drive, Novell brings him to the directory TEMP. To add more mapped drives, repeat these preceding steps, starting with step 3.

To delete a mapped drive, go to the Drive Mappings menu, highlight the drive you want to delete, and press the Delete key. You now see a Novell prompt asking if you want to delete drive mapping. Highlight the Yes and press Enter. The mapped drive has now been deleted.

To delete several mapped drives, mark them using your Mark key (press F1 twice to verify the Mark key for your computer) and press the Delete key. You are asked to confirm the deletion.

To edit a mapped drive, go to the Drive Mappings menu. Highlight the mapped drive you wish to edit and make changes using the keyboard. Novell menus assume that you are in an insert mode.

The creations, deletions, and/or additions made with Session are temporary. When you log out of Novell, they disappear. If you want changes to be permanent, you must put them in your login script.

CREATING, DELETING, AND EDITING SEARCH DRIVES IN SESSION

You can also create, edit, or delete search drive maps in session. At the DOS prompt, type SESSION and Enter. When the Session menu appears on the screen, highlight Search Drive Mappings and press Enter. For all creating, deleting, and editing Search Drive Mappings, follow the same steps you used in "Creating, Deleting and Editing Mapped Drives in Session."

LOGIN SCRIPT COMMANDS

The following commands are available to customize your login scripts:

Attach	External Program Execution (#)
Break	Fire Phasers
Comspec	IF . . . THEN
Display and Fdisplay	Include
DOS Break	Machine Name
DOS Set	Map
DOS Verify	Pause
Drive	Remark
Exit	Write

Following is the purpose of each command, as well as the syntax required to use the command and an example of how the command works.

Attach

Syntax   ATTACH *file server*[username;[*password*]]

Purpose   Attach is used when you have more than one file server. The command allows you to connect to additional file servers during the login process.

Example   ATTACH FS2/JOHN;BASEBALL
This command attaches John to File Server 2. Because his user name and password were included in the Attach command, Novell did not ask for this information during login. If the name and password are not included, Novell requests them during the login process.

Break

Syntax   BREAK ON
             BREAK OFF

Purpose   Break On and Break Off allows you to enter a command in the login script that will allow a user to stop the execution of the login script during the login process (Break On) or prevent the user from doing so (Break Off). If the Break On command has been entered in the login script, the user can press Ctrl/C or Ctrl/Break at any point in the login process to abort the execution of the login script.

Example   By placing Break On in John's Login Script, the Supervisor has given John the option of aborting the execution of his Login Script.

Comspec

Syntax   COMSPEC=Sn:filename

The n represents the search drive. This search drive should be the same search drive set up for DOS.

Purpose   Comspec is used to specify the directory containing the DOS command processor, COMMAND.COM. Some application programs will not operate correctly if Comspec is not in the Login Script. Normally, Comspec is placed in the System Login Script.

Example   The following mapping is in ABC's System Login Script:

        MAP S2:=SYS:DOS
        COMSPEC=S2:COMMAND.COM

The first line (MAP S2:=SYS:DOS) maps DOS to search drive 2.

The second line (COMSPEC=S2:COMMAND.COM) directs the system to the location (the DOS directory) of COMMAND.COM.

Display and Fdisplay

Syntax DISPLAY [*directory*]*filename*
FDISPLAY [*directory*]*filename*

Purpose Display and Fdisplay are used to display the contents of text files during the login process. If you use Display, any formatting in the file is displayed as well as the text. If you use Fdisplay, the formatting is filtered out and only the text will be displayed.

Example FDISPLAY SYS3:WP/NEWS/NEWS.TXT

This message displays the contents of the file NEWS.TXT during the login process. For example, the supervisor can update the file in order to inform the staff of a meeting that day.

DOS Break On and Dos Break Off

Syntax DOS BREAK ON
DOS BREAK OFF

Purpose These commands determine whether the user can interrupt any DOS commands or programs after the login process is complete. These commands are not interchangeable with the Break commands. The default command is DOS Break Off.

Example By entering DOS Break On in a blank line of a user's Login Script, that user is able to use Ctrl/Break to terminate a program or DOS command after login is complete. This command prevents premature termination of the login process.

For more information on the DOS Break command, refer to your DOS manual.

DOS Set

Syntax SET *name* = "*value*"

Purpose The DOS Set command allows the user to set a variable to a specified value in the DOS environment.

Example   ABC's System Login Script has the following SET command:

SET PROMPT="pg"

This command instructs Novell to show the current DOS directory at your prompt. The "$P" displays the drive and directory; "$G" displays a > character.

For more information about available SET names and values, see your DOS manual.

The DOS environment space is limited. If you use too many Set commands, you can run out of room in your DOS environment. To learn how to control the environment space in your computer, see the Shell command in your DOS manual.

DOS Verify

Syntax   DOS VERIFY ON
DOS VERIFY OFF

Purpose   The DOS Verify command verifies that data has been correctly copied to a local drive.

Example   DOS Verify On entered on a blank line in your Login Script will verify that data has been properly copied to a local drive when using the DOS COPY command.

If DOS Verify Off has been entered in your Login Script, you can still verify the copy by using the /v qualifier with the DOS COPY command or the Novell Ncopy command.

For further information on DOS copy command options, refer to your DOS manual.

Further information on the Novell Ncopy command is in Chapter 1.

Drive

Syntax   DRIVE *n*:

where *n* = a letter.

Purpose   The Drive command allows users to change their default drive when they log in. If there is no Drive command in the Login Script, the system defaults to the first network drive.

Example   By entering the following command in a user's Login Script, that user will always default to the directory L:\BOOK upon login:

DRIVE L:

Please note that in order for this command to work the specified drive must be mapped in the Login Script on any line preceding the Drive command. Consequently, for the above DRIVE L: command to work, the following command must be placed on a line above it in the Login Script:

MAP L:=SYS:BOOK

Exit

Syntax   EXIT
EXIT *"filename"*

Purpose   The EXIT command allows the user to terminate execution of the login commands and execute .COM, .EXE, and .BAT commands, and DOS internal commands.

Do not use this command to exit to a TSR program.

When this command is entered into a Login Script any commands entered after the EXIT command are ignored.

Example   If you want the Login Script to take a user to a menu screen called Main the following command would be entered on the last line of the Login Script:

EXIT "Menu Main"

This command would bring the user directly to the menu called Main.

The EXIT command can be used with IF . . . THEN identifier variables.

External Program Execution (#)

Syntax   #[*directory*]*filename parameter line*

Purpose   The External Program Execution (#) command is used to execute a command that is external to the Login Script. You must specify the correct path and file name. The user must also have proper security rights to that path and file name. Finally, your computer must have sufficient memory to execute the command.

Do not use this command to execute to a TSR program.

Example Using WordPerfect, a user has created a file called CALENDAR. He uses this file to list his daily appointments and keeps it in his user directory. The following commands are entered in his login script so he can access this file during the login process.

```
IF "%2" = "CAL" THEN BEGIN
#SYS:WP/WP CALENDAR
END
```

This command directs Novell to exit temporarily from the login script, execute WordPerfect, and, using WordPerfect's startup option (WP [filename]), to immediately retrieve the file calendar. After the user exits from WordPerfect, the login script process will continue.

In order for the External Program Execution command to work, Novell must be able to find both the directory and the execute file.

In the above example, it was necessary to use the Drive command to make the user's directory the default directory. We also had to set up a search drive in the Map commands for the program WordPerfect.

Fire Phasers

Syntax FIRE PHASERS *n* TIMES

where *n* equals the number of times.

Purpose This command allows you to fire phasers (which sound like the phasers in Star Trek).

Example Place Fire Phasers 5 Times command at the beginning of your Login Script Novell to give you the phaser sound 5 times upon login.

You can also use this command in conjunction with a conditional command to fire phasers, if certain conditions exist. See the If . . . Then commands in this chapter for more information about conditional commands.

If . . . Then

Syntax IF *condition(s)* THEN *command*

Purpose This command is used to execute commands during the login process when certain conditions are met.

Table 4-1. IF . . . THEN Condition Identifier Variables

Command	Description
HOUR	Hour of day or night (1–12)
HOUR24	(00–23)
MINUTE	(00–59)
SECOND	(00–59)
AM_PM	(am or pm)
MONTH	(month number (01–12)
MONTH_NAME	(January, etc.)
DAY	(01–31)
NDAY_OF_WEEK	(1–7, Sunday=1)
YEAR	1990, etc.
SHORT_YEAR	90, etc.
DAY_OF_WEEK	Monday, etc.
LOGIN_NAME	John, etc.
FULL_NAME	John Smith (from SYSCON files)
STATION	Workstation 1, etc.
P_STATION	Physical Station (12 hex digits)
GREETING_TIME	Morning, afternoon, evening.
SHELL_TYPE	Shell type number (0, 27, etc.)
NEW_MAIL	YES or NO indicating whether new mail has arrived.
OS	Workstation Operating System; e.g., MS-DOS, etc.
OS_Version	Version of Workstation DOS, V.3.30, etc.
MACHINE	The machine which the shell was written for, IBM_PC, etc.
SMACHINE	Short name (IBM, etc.)
ERROR_LEVEL	A value, i.e., 0 (no errors) or any number other than 0 (errors)
MEMBER_OF_ GROUPNAME	Group name (as defined in SYSCON)

Example   In ABC's Login Script we used the following command:

```
IF DAY_OF_WEEK = "Monday" THEN WRITE "\n\ "It's
    Monday––Have a Nice Week \"\n\n"
```

This command instructed Novell to execute a command (THEN WRITE) if a specific condition was met (IF DAY_OF_WEEK="Monday").

Table 4-1 shows the Identifier Variables, reecognized by Novell when naming a condition.

NOTE: ERROR_LEVEL and MEMBER_OF_GROUPNAME are new identifier variables found only in Novell NetWare version 2.11 or higher.

The above variables meet the IF segment of the IF . . . THEN statement. There are six possible relationships that meet the relationship segment of the statement: equal to; not equal to; greater than; less than; greater than or equal to; less than or equal to.

Equal and Not Equal relationships are represented as follows:

Equal	*Not Equal*
IS	IS NOT
=	!=
==	<>
EQUALS	DOES NOT EQUAL
	NOT EQUAL TO

Other relationships can be represented this way:

Symbol	*Meaning*
>	IS GREATER THAN
<	IS LESS THAN
>=	IS GREATER THAN OR EQUAL TO
<=	IS LESS THAN OR EQUAL TO

Conditions can be joined with commas or the word AND to be formed into compound conditions:

```
IF MEMBER OF "Sales" AND DAY_OF_WEEK="Tuesday"
THEN WRITE "\n\"DON'T FORGET!!! TUESDAY SALES
MEETING. \"\n\n"
```

The % symbol followed by a number in a Login Script command is replaced by the corresponding parameter in the command. The first parameter after LOGIN is %1.

For example in the command:

IF "%2" = "CAL" THEN BEGIN

the following values apply:

LOGIN JOHN(%1)   CAL (%2)

After entering the *IF* and (*relationship*) segments of the *IF . . . THEN* command, the command following the THEN segment must be entered:

IF DAY_OF_WEEK="Monday" THEN WRITE

Include

Syntax   INCLUDE [*directory*]*filename*

Purpose   This command instructs Novell to print to screen text files not included in the Login Script during the login process. These text files must contain valid script commands, i.e., WRITE. Any text editor can be used to write the file. INCLUDE nesting can be 10 levels deep.

Example   If a supervisor needs to broadcast a message to each user he/she could include the following command in the System Login Script:

INCLUDE SYS:PUBLIC   MESSAGE

The text file MESSAGE would be found in the PUBLIC directory and would contain the command WRITE followed by the text in quotes:

WRITE "MEETING TODAY AT 10:00 IN
THE CONFERENCE ROOM"

Users must have Open and Read rights (see Chapter 3 for more information on Trustee Rights) to access the file.

Be sure to include the PAUSE command on the line immediately after the Include command. This keeps the text on the screen until the user hits a key instructing the login script to continue executing.

Machine Name

Syntax   MACHINE NAME = "*name*"
              MACHINE = "*name*"

Purpose   This command sets the machine name of the station to a specified name. The machine name may contain up to 15 characters. This command is necessary to run some programs under PC DOS.

Example   MACHINE NAME = "IBM_PC"

Map

Syntax   Table 4-2 shows the syntax and gives a brief description of each form of the MAP Syntax.

Table 4-2. Map Command Syntax

Command	Description
MAP	Displays current map drives for all defined drives on a workstation.
MAP *drive:*	Displays current mapping for the drive specified.
MAP *drive:=directory*	Maps the specified drive to the given directory (list full directory path, i.e., map s:=sys:user/mary).
MAP *directory*	Maps the default drive to the specified directory.
MAP *drive:=*	Maps the specified drive to the directory that the default drive is mapped to.
MAP *drive:=drive:*	Maps the first drive to the same directory that the second drive has been mapped to.
MAP INSERT *search drive:=directory*	Maps a new search drive using the next available letter.
MAP DEL *drive:*	Deletes a MAP definition.
MAP REM *drive:*	Same as MAP DEL.
MAP DISPLAY ON	Instructs Novell to display all drive mappings during the execution of the login script.
MAP DISPLAY OFF	Instructs Novell to turn off the display of all drive mappings during the execution of the login script.

Purpose   MAP commands in login scripts permanently map drives to a directory. This avoids the need to map drives everytime you log in.

Example   See the examples with the explanations of mapped drives earlier in this chapter.

Pause

Syntax   PAUSE
WAIT

Purpose   This command instructs Novell to pause during the execution of the Login Script execution. The user is then instructed to Strike a Key when ready to continue the execution of the login script.

Example   Pause can be used when a message is displayed. This allows the user to have time to read the message before the login script continues execution.

Remark

Syntax   REMARK [*text*]
* [*text*]
; [*text*]
REM [*text*]

Purpose   Remark is useful for including explanations to yourself about commands you have put in the login script. These remarks do not appear on screen when the login script is executed.
Remark or Rem, as well as the "*" and ";" must be the first item entered on the line.

Example   Remark This external command will bring John to Word-Perfect upon login.

Write

Syntax   WRITE [*text string(s)*]
WRITE [*identifier(s)*]

Text strings must be enclosed in quotation marks ("). In addition, the following super-characters can be used:

\r   carriage return
\n   new line

    \"   embedded quotation mark
    \7   sound a beep

Multiple text strings and identifiers can be entered if each is separated by a semicolon (;).

See Table 4-1 for a list of variables you can use with the Write command.

Purpose   This command is used to write messages to the screen during the login process.

Example   WRITE " \n \n Good %GREETING_TIME,
         %LOGIN _NAME"

This command skips two lines on the screen and inserts the following message when John logs in under the login name John:

    Good Morning, John

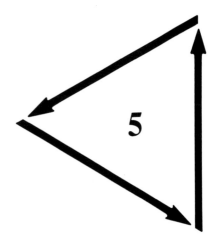

5

Security and Supervisor Options

A SUPERVISOR or supervisor equivalent is a user with complete rights to every application on the network. This person is responsible for overseeing network security.

Security on a network operates on several levels. One level of security concerns hardware fault tolerance and troubleshooting. This material is covered in Chapters 8, 9, and 10. Another level of security concerns directory and file access. This is covered in Chapter 3. A third level of security involves the interface of users with the operating system. This involves matters such as accounting, passwords, time restrictions, account restrictions, and other features covering operating system security. Security for the operating system is set in the Syscon menu through features in Accounting, Supervisor Options, and User Information. This chapter will cover all elements concerning operating system security.

USER SECURITY

Each time a user is created in Novell, an account is set up for that user. The supervisor must then set the security restrictions for that user. Security restrictions are set in Syscon. To set security restrictions for a user, do the following:

1. Type SYSCON and press Enter.

2. Highlight User Information and press Enter.

3. Highlight the user you are setting restrictions for and press enter.

The User Information menu (shown in Fig. 5-1) appears. The options appearing on this screen are explained in the following paragraphs.

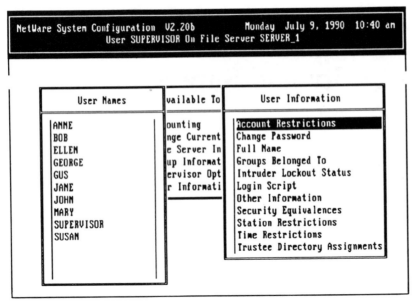

Fig. 5-1. User information menu

Account Restrictions

The Account Restrictions feature sets up security restrictions for each user. Default values can be set in the Supervisor Options feature of Syscon, covered later in this chapter.

Individual restrictions can be set up through the Account Restrictions menu accessed in User Information. If you highlight Account Restrictions in the User Information (see Fig. 5-2), you can set the following account restrictions:

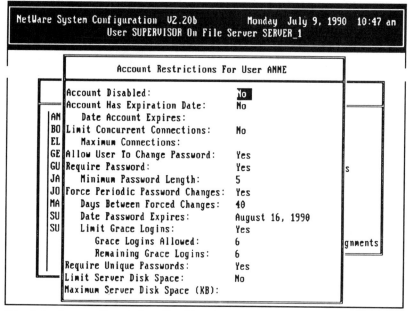

```
NetWare System Configuration  V2.20b          Monday  July 9, 1990  10:47 an
                    User SUPERVISOR On File Server SERVER_1
```

```
              Account Restrictions For User ANNE

      Account Disabled:                      No
      Account Has Expiration Date:           No
AN        Date Account Expires:
BO    Limit Concurrent Connections:         No
EL        Maximum Connections:
GE    Allow User To Change Password:        Yes
GU    Require Password:                     Yes              s
JA        Minimum Password Length:          5
JO    Force Periodic Password Changes:      Yes
MA        Days Between Forced Changes:      40
SU        Date Password Expires:            August 16, 1990
SU        Limit Grace Logins:               Yes
              Grace Logins Allowed:         6
              Remaining Grace Logins:       6              gnments
      Require Unique Passwords:             Yes
      Limit Server Disk Space:              No
      Maximum Server Disk Space (KB):
```

Fig. 5-2. Account Restrictions For User Anne.

Account Disabled   This feature allows the supervisor to temporarily disable an account without deleting it from the system. This is useful for users who require access to their account only for specific time periods. By changing this response to Yes, the account will be closed temporarily until it is required again, at which time the supervisor can change the response back to No.

Account Has Expiration Date   This feature is used for setting up a temporary account. After the date specified, the account is closed and the user cannot log in.

Limit Concurrent Connections   This feature limits the number of workstations a user can log in to. The default is set for an unlimited number of workstations. To set restrictions, change this value from NO to YES. The Maximum Connections value can be set from 1 to 100.

NOTE: This feature can be affected by shells such as Microsoft Windows if they limit the number of workstations a user can log in to. Such software limitations will override the Novell setting in this menu.

Allow User to Change Password   This feature determines whether or not the user can change his own password. If the response is set to No, only the supervisor can change the password. This feature is usually used to protect public accounts that are accessed by several users, such as TEMP.

Require Password   It is absolutely essential to the security of a network to require passwords for users. Otherwise any user can access a level of security on the network just by logging in using the name of a user who has that level of security.

If you answer Yes to this feature, the system will automatically set the minimum length of five characters for the password. The supervisor can change this minimum length in the Minimum Password Length field. The maximum length of a password is 128 characters.

Force Periodic Password Changes   This feature, when set to Yes, requires users to change their passwords periodically. If you require a password and allow users to change their own passwords, this feature is automatically set to Yes and requires password changes every 40 days. The supervisor can change the number of days required between password changes or can set this feature to No so that periodic password changes are not required.

Once the number of days between forced changes are set, the system automatically shows the Date Password Expires. On that date, the user will be prompted to enter a new password. Once the new password is entered, the Date Password Expires is automatically recalculated.

Limit Grace Logins   This feature limits the number of times a user can login with an expired password. If the user does not change his password and exceeds the grace limit, his account is disabled and he is locked out of the system.

If this feature is set to No, the user will be prompted to change his password every time he logs in, but he will not be locked out of the system because his password has expired.

Require Unique Passwords   This feature requires users to change to a different password when their old password has expired. Otherwise he can just use the same password each time a periodic password change is forced.

The system will remember a user's last eight passwords. This means that if this feature is set to Yes, a user must use at least eight unique passwords before he can start using them over again.

Disk Resource Limitation   This option only appears if the Disk Resource Limitation option was selected during the installation process. It is used to limit the amount of file server disk space available to each user.

A default can be set for all users (see "System Default Account Restrictions" in this chapter) or each user can be assigned a different amount of available space.

If you change this feature to Yes, you should enter the maximum amount of disk space available to the user in the Maximum Disk Space Field. This amount should be entered in kilobytes (KB).

When you have completed all changes in this menu, press Escape to save the changes and return to the User Information menu.

Change Password

This feature is used to assign or change a user's password. Each time a user is added to the system, the supervisor should assign him a password. If the user has been granted rights to change his own password (see above, "Account Restrictions" "Allow User to Change Password"), then the user can change only his own password. Only the supervisor can change a user's password if this right has not been granted.

To change a password, highlight Change Password and press Enter. Type in the password in the Enter New Password box. The characters will not be displayed as you type. You will then be asked to confirm the password by typing it in a second time.

Full Name

This field is used by some utilities to identify the user by full name rather than just the login name. It is used for reporting purposes only.

Groups Belonged To

This feature allows the user to view the groups he belongs to. It also allows the supervisor to add or delete groups from a user. For a complete explanation of Groups and this feature, see Chapter 3.

Intruder Lockout Status

The Supervisor Options menu in Syscon allows the supervisor to lock out an account after a certain number of unsuccessful login attempts. Intruder Lockout Status allows you to view the lockout status of an account. This feature does not work unless Accounting has been installed.

Login Script

This feature allows either a user or the supervisor to create a user Login Script. User Login Scripts and the use of this feature are covered completely in Chapter 4.

Other Information

This feature provides general information about each user, including last login date and time, console operator status (see "Supervisor Options" in this chapter), maximum server disk space usage set in Account Restrictions (previously discussed in this chapter), disk space in use, and the user's bindery ID number.

Security Equivalences

This feature allows the supervisor to assign a user the same security as another user or group. For example, the supervisor sets up a group called Accounting with certain rights in the accounting directories. The supervisor can then make all users who need these rights a security equivalent to Accounting. For more information on groups, users, and trustee rights, see Chapter 3.

To assign a user's security equivalence, follow these steps:

1. Type SYSCON and press Enter at the DOS prompt. The Available Topics menu is displayed.

2. Highlight User Information and press Enter. A user list is displayed.

3. Highlight the user you want to assign security equivalence to and press Enter. The User Information menu is displayed.

4. Highlight Security Equivalences and press Enter. The user's security equivalences are displayed.

5. Press Insert. The Other Users and Groups list is displayed.

6. Highlight the user or group that you want to make the user equivalent to and press Enter.

The supervisor can also use this feature to delete a user's security equivalence. To delete a user's security equivalence, follow steps 1–4 above. In the Security Equivalences list, highlight the group or user you want to delete and press Delete. You are now asked to confirm the deletion.

Station Restrictions

This feature allows the supervisor to limit the location of the workstations a user may log in from. For example, you may want a user to log in only from the workstation in his office. The default sets no workstation restrictions.

To set station restrictions, it is necessary to know the network and node address of each workstation. You can obtain the address of a workstation by logging into that workstation and typing USERLIST/A at the DOS prompt.

To assign station restrictions follow these steps:

1. At the DOS prompt, type SYSCON and press Enter. The Available Topics menu is displayed.

2. Highlight User Information and press Enter. A user list is displayed.

3. Highlight the user you wish to set station restrictions for and press Enter. The User Information menu will be displayed.

4. Highlight Station Restrictions and press Enter. The Allowed Login Addresses list is displayed. If this list is empty, the user can log in from any workstation.

5. Press Insert. The Network Address box is displayed. Type the network address(es) of the workstation(s) you wish to restrict the user to and press Enter. You are now asked to confirm your choice.

The supervisor can also delete workstation restrictions. To delete a restriction, follow steps 1–4 above. In the Allowed Login Addresses list, highlight the address of the station you want to delete and press Delete. You are now asked to confirm the deletion.

Time Restrictions

This feature allows the supervisor to restrict the days and hours during which users can log in to the system. The default is set for no time restrictions. For example, you want to prevent Anne from accessing the system of Saturday or Sunday.

To assign time restrictions to a user follow these steps:

1. At the DOS prompt, type SYSCON and press Enter. The Available Topics menu will be displayed.

2. Highlight User Information and press Enter. A user list will be displayed.

3. Highlight the user (Anne) you want to place time restrictions on and press Enter. You can use the Mark key to assign the same time restrictions to multiple users. (Press F1 to confirm the Mark key on your computer.) The User Information menu is displayed.

4. Highlight Time Restrictions and press Enter. The Allowed Login Times For User Anne screen will be displayed as shown in Fig. 5-3.

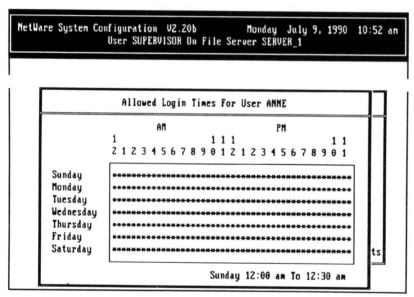

Fig. 5-3. Allowed Login Times For User Anne.

5. Using the Mark key, mark the blocks of time during which you do not want to allow the user to access the system (press F1 to find the Mark key for your computer) and press Delete. Highlight Yes and press Enter to confirm the deletion.

6. To insert blocks of time in the Allowed Login Times for User Anne screen, bring your cursor to where you want to start marking, press the Mark key, use your cursor arrow keys to mark the segment of time you wish to insert, and press Insert.

The supervisor can modify the system default time restrictions by setting them in the Default Time Restrictions feature in Supervisor Options (covered later in this chapter).

Trustee Assignments

This feature allows the supervisor to set user's trustee rights to files and directories. For a complete explanation of how this feature works see Chapter 3. Assigning Trustee Rights to Users.

SUPERVISOR OPTIONS

The Supervisor Options menu is found in SYSCON. This menu contains features that allow the supervisor to set certain defaults for the entire system.

Default Account Balance/Restrictions

This feature allows the supervisor to set default Account Restrictions. These restrictions will only apply to users created after the restrictions have been set up. To set default Account Restrictions follow these steps:

1. Type SYSCON and press Enter at the DOS prompt. The Available Topics menu will be displayed.

2. Highlight Supervisor Options and press Enter. The Supervisor Options menu is displayed. See Fig. 5-4.

3. Highlight Default Account Balance/Restrictions and press Enter. The Default Account Balance/Restrictions menu is now on the screen. Figure 5-5 shows this menu.

4. Change the defaults to restrictions you wish to apply to all users. A complete explanation of each restriction is previously explained in the section entitled User Security, Account Restrictions in this chapter.

Default Time Restrictions

This feature is used to set default time restrictions for all users. To set default time restrictions, follow these steps:

1. At the DOS prompt, type SYSCON and press Enter. The Available Topics menu will be displayed.

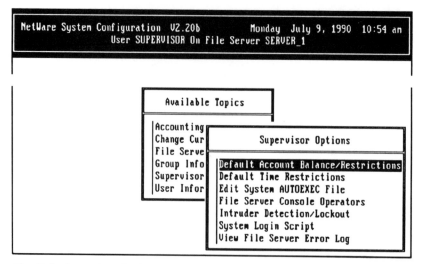

Fig. 5-4. Supervisor Options.

```
NetWare System Configuration  V2.20b          Monday  July 9, 1990  10:57 an
                    User SUPERVISOR On File Server SERVER_1

        ┌─────────────────────────────────────────────┐
        │        Default Account Balance/Restrictions  │
        │                                              │
        │ Account Has Expiration Date:    No           │
        │    Date Account Expires:                     │
        │ Limit Concurrent Connections:   No           │
        │    Maximum Connections:                      │
        │ Require Password:               No           │
        │    Minimum Password Length:            strictions
        │ Force Periodic Password Changes:             │
        │    Days Between Forced Changes:              │
        │    Limit Grace Logins:                 ors
        │       Grace Logins Allowed:                  │
        │ Require Unique Passwords:                    │
        │ Account Balance:                0            │
        │ Allow Unlimited Credit:         No           │
        │    Low Balance Limit:           0            │
        │ Limit Server Disk Space:        No           │
        │ Maximum Server Disk Space (KB):              │
        └─────────────────────────────────────────────┘
```

Fig. 5-5. Default Account Balance/Restrictions

2. Highlight Supervisor Options and press Enter. The Supervisor Options menu will be displayed.

3. Highlight Default Time Restrictions and press Enter. The Default Time Restrictions, Fig. 5-6, screen will be displayed.

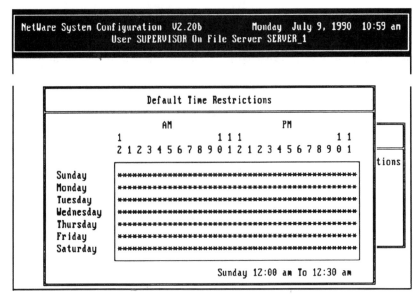

Fig. 5-6. Default Time Restrictions

4. Set default time restrictions following the steps previously described in User Security, Time Restrictions.

Edit System AUTOEXEC File

The AUTOEXEC.SYS file is used to store console commands that are to be executed each time the file server is booted up. While any console command (except DOWN) can be stored in the AUTOEXEC.SYS file, this feature is usually used for printer mappings.

When Novell is installed each printer is automatically assigned to a queue. (Queues are identified in Chapter 7. Queue assignments can be viewed using the List All Print Queues console command explained in Chapter 9 or through the Pconsole menu explained in Chapter 7.) Additional queues can then later be permanently mapped to printers in the AUTOEXEC.SYS file using the console command Add.

When mapping printers in the AUTOEXEC.SYS file, be sure to include the default mapping set up by the system as well as new mappings. For example, let us assume a network was set up with five printers. The printers and queues would be mapped as follows:

PRINTER0	PRINTQ_0
PRINTER1	PRINTQ_1
PRINTER2	PRINTQ_2
PRINTER3	PRINTQ_3
PRINTER4	PRINTQ_4

In addition, two queues have been created called Sales and Accounting (see Chapter 7, "Creating a Print Queue") that are to be mapped to PRINTER0 and PRINTER1, respectively.

In order for the printers to function properly, it is also necessary to include spooler mappings for every queue. This is done by inserting the console command Change Spooler Mappings (see Chapter 9) into the AUTOEXEC.SYS file.

After the server boots up, the supervisor would like to clear the monitor. This is accomplished by inserting the console command OFF in the AUTOEXEC.SYS file.

We are now going to create an AUTOEXEC.SYS file to accomplish these requirements.

1. Type SYSCON and press Enter at the DOS prompt. The Available Topics menu is displayed.

2. Highlight Supervisor Options and press Enter. The Supervisor Options menu is displayed.

3. Highlight Edit System AUTOEXEC File and press Enter. The System AUTOEXEC File entry box is displayed.

4. Type in the commands you want to be executed each time the file server is booted up.

```
P 0 ADD PRINTQ_0
P 0 ADD SALES
P 1 ADD PRINTQ_1
P 1 ADD ACCOUNTING
P 2 ADD PRINTQ_2
P 3 ADD PRINTQ_3
P 4 ADD PRINTQ_4
S 0 PRINTQ_0
```

S 0 SALES
S 1 PRINTQ_1
S 1 ACCOUNTING
S 2 PRINTQ_2
S 3 PRINTQ_3
S 4 PRINTQ_4
OFF

Your System AUTOEXEC File entry box should look as shown in Fig. 5-7.

5. Press Escape and then Enter on YES to save the changes.

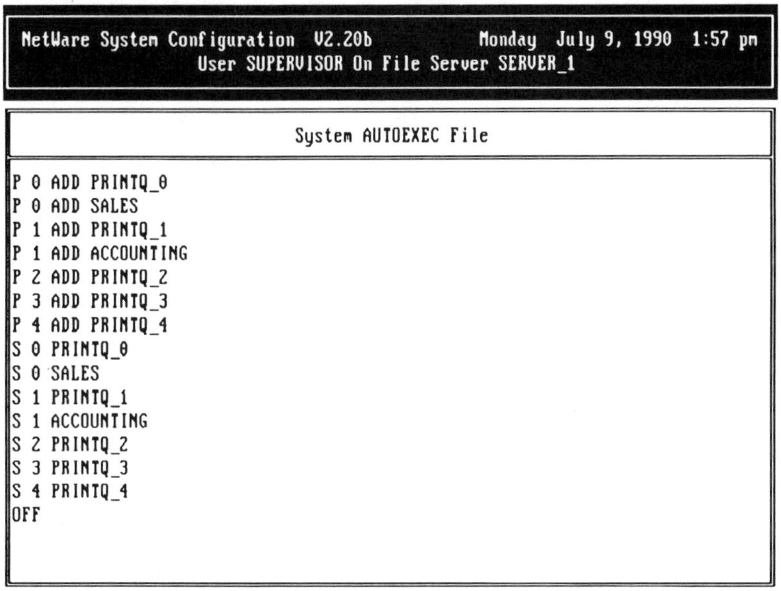

```
 NetWare System Configuration  V2.20b          Monday  July 9, 1990  1:57 pm
                     User SUPERVISOR On File Server SERVER_1

                             System AUTOEXEC File

P 0 ADD PRINTQ_0
P 0 ADD SALES
P 1 ADD PRINTQ_1
P 1 ADD ACCOUNTING
P 2 ADD PRINTQ_2
P 3 ADD PRINTQ_3
P 4 ADD PRINTQ_4
S 0 PRINTQ_0
S 0 SALES
S 1 PRINTQ_1
S 1 ACCOUNTING
S 2 PRINTQ_2
S 3 PRINTQ_3
S 4 PRINTQ_4
OFF
```

Fig. 5-7. System AUTOEXEC File

File Server Console Operators

This feature allows the supervisor to determine which users and groups are file server console operators. File server console operators are able to make system changes using the Fconsole menu utility. For a complete explanation of Fconsole, see Chapter 8.

To add or delete a file server console operator follow these steps:

1. Type SYSCON and press Enter at the DOS prompt. The Available Topics menu will be displayed.

2. Highlight Supervisor Options and press Enter. The Supervisor Options menu will be displayed.

3. Highlight File Server Console Operators and press Enter. The File Server Console Operators list appears, as shown in Fig. 5-8 listing any users or groups that are console operators.

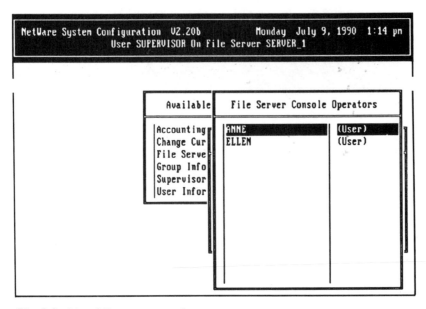

Fig. 5-8. List of file server console operators

4. To add console operators, press Insert. The Other Users and Groups list is displayed.

5. Highlight the user or group you wish to add as a console operator and press Enter.

6. To delete console operators, follow steps 1 through 3 above. In the File Server Console Operators list, highlight the user or group you wish to delete and press Delete. You are now asked to confirm the deletion.

Intruder Detection/Lockout

This feature, if activated, will keep track of any attempt to log in with an incorrect password more than the allotted number of times. The supervisor can also instruct the system to close the account for a designated time period after a specified number of unsuccessful login attempts. To activate the Intruder Detection/Lockout feature, follow these steps:

1. Type SYSCON and press Enter at the DOS prompt. The Available Topics menu is displayed.

2. Highlight Supervisor Options and press Enter. The Supervisor Options menu is displayed.

3. Highlight Intruder Detection/Lockout and press Enter. The Intruder Detection/Lockout screen is displayed, as seen in Fig. 5-9.

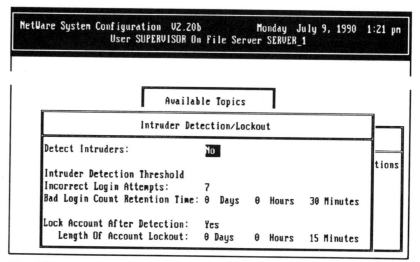

Fig. 5-9. Intruder detection/lockout screen

4. Change the Detect Intruders: option to Yes and press Enter.

5. Set the Incorrect Login Attempts: option to the number of incorrect login attempts the server will allow before assuming an intruder is trying to log in.

6. Set the Bad Login Count Retention Time: option. This feature will determine how long the file server will keep track of an unsuccessful login attempt before resetting.

7. Set the Lock Account After Detection: option. If you set this feature to Yes, the account will be locked after the specified number of unsuccessful login attempts (set in the Incorrect Login Attempts: field).

8. If you answered Yes to the Lock Account After Detection: option, set the Length Of Account Lockout: option to the amount of time the account will be locked after an intruder is detected.

System Login Script

This feature allows the supervisor to customize the network by sending instructions to each workstation during the login process. For a complete explanation of Login Scripts, see Chapter 4.

View File Server Error Log

This feature allows the supervisor to view and erase any errors recorded in the file server's error log. The list includes any errors detected since the log was last cleared, the date, time and nature of the error. To view the file server's error log follow these steps:

1. Type SYSCON and press Enter at the DOS prompt. The Available Topics menu is displayed.

2. Highlight Supervisor Options and press Enter. The Supervisor Options menu is displayed.

3. Highlight View File Server Error Log and press Enter. The File Server Error Log screen appears listing any new error messages. Use the arrow keys to scroll through the list. A complete explanation of all error messages can be found in the NetWare Systems Messages Manual.

4. To exit the log press Escape. You are now asked if you want to clear the log. If you say Yes, the error messages will be erased from the log. If you say No, the error messages will be retained and can be read the next time you view the log.

WHAT IS THE ACCOUNTING OPTION?

The accounting option in Syscon is a method by which the file server keeps track of services used and charges for them. There are five different type of services for which the file server can charge.

Blocks Read Charge Rates

This option allows you to charge a user whenever he or she reads from the disk. You can specify the charge in 30-minute increments. The charge is assigned per block read, with one block being equal to 4096 bytes, or 4KB.

Blocks Written Charge Rates

This option allows you to charge a user whenever he or she writes to the disk. As with blocks read, you can specify the charge in 30-minute increments. The charge is assigned per block written, with one block being equal to 4096 bytes, or 4KB.

Connect Time Charge Rates

This option allows you to charge a user for the amount of time he or she is logged in to the server. You can specify the amount charged by the half-hour. Connect time charge rates are by the minute.

Disk Storage Charge Rates

This option allows you to charge for each block that is stored by a user per day. Just as in the other charge rates, you can assign a charge rate for each half hour.

Service Requests Charge Rates

This option allows you to charge a user for each request made of the file server. You can assign a charge rate for each half-hour.

ACCOUNTING REPORTS

The file server will track any or all of these charges and record them in the NET$ACCT.DAT file located in the SYS:SYSTEM directory. You can then run Atotal from the SYS:SYSTEM directory for a printout of charge accrued by the server. For a more detailed report, you can run

Paudit which will give you a chronological list of all accounting functions, including logins, logouts and a list of all charges made to each user. Both Atotal and Paudit may be directed to a file and then printed at a later time. To accomplish this do the following:

1. Type PAUDIT (or ATOTAL) > filename to direct the data to a file.

2. Type NPRINT *filename* [option(s)] to print the file. (Nprint is covered in chapter 7.)

3. Type TYPE *filename* | MORE to print to the screen one page at a time.

Because Paudit contains massive amounts of data, after you print out the information contained in Atotal and Paudit, you may want to delete the NET$ACCT.DAT file. The information will begin to accumulate again and will start at the point from which you deleted NET$ACCT.DAT.

CAUTION: If your accounting or billing program uses the NET$ACCT.DAT file, do not erase the old NET$ACCT.DAT file until you are certain that erasing it will not cause problems with accounting or billing.

HOW TO INSTALL ACCOUNTING

The accounting option was installed with your Novell system. Before you can use it, however, you must tell Novell you want it to be activated. To activate accounting, do the following:

1. Type SYSCON and press Enter at the DOS prompt. You are in the Available Topics menu.

2. Highlight Accounting and press Enter. You see the Install Accounting confirmation screen.

3. Highlight Yes.

When you activate accounting, the current file server will automatically be able to charge for services used. If you add more servers to the system, you must activate the accounting option in order to authorize the servers to charge users for their services. To authorize a new server to charge for its services, do the following:

1. Type SYSCON and press Enter at the DOS prompt. You are in the Available Topics menu.

2. Highlight Accounting and press Enter. You are in the Accounting menu.

3. Highlight Accounting Servers and press Enter. You see a list of all servers that are authorized to charge for services.

4. Press Insert and you are in the Select Server Type menu. This will list all of the types of servers recognized by Syscon that can charge for services.

5. Highlight the type of server you wish to authorize and press Enter. You are now in the Other Servers menu.

6. Highlight the server you wish to authorize and charge for services and press Enter.

7. If you wish to authorize more than one server, use your Mark key (press F1 twice to verify the Mark key for your computer) for each and press Enter.

8. Press Esc to exit.

HOW TO DELETE A SERVER FROM ACCOUNTING

You can delete a server from Accounting as follows:

1. Type SYSCON and press Enter at the DOS prompt. You are in the Available Topics menu.

2. Highlight Accounting and press Enter. You see a list of servers authorized to charge for services.

3. Highlight the server you wish to delete and press Delete. If you want delete more than one server, use your Mark key (press F1 twice on your computer to verify the Mark key) to select each one and press Delete. The Delete Account Server confirmation screen appears.

4. Highlight Yes and press Enter. The Accounting Servers list no longer contains these servers.

HOW TO DEACTIVATE THE ACCOUNTING OPTION

Before you can deactivate the accounting option, you must delete all servers. To do this, follow steps 1 through 4 in How to Delete a Server from Accounting. When all servers have been deleted, press Esc. You will see the Do You Wish To Remove Accounting confirmation screen. Highlight Yes and press Enter. You are back in the Available Topics menu and accounting has been deactivated.

HOW TO SET CHARGE RATES

Before you set charge rates, you must determine the amount you wish to charge users on your system for each of the services for which they are being charged. It is helpful to track the services being used for a period of time (perhaps a month) in order to estimate how much each service is being used. In order for the system to record usage for each service, you must first assign a charge rate. For the purposes of establishing an estimate of use for each service, assign a charge rate of 1/1. Do the following to accomplish this:

1. Type SYSCON and press Enter at the DOS prompt. You are in the Available Topics menu.

2. Highlight Accounting and press Enter. You are now in the Accounting menu.

3. Highlight Blocks Read Charge Rates and press Enter. You see the Blocks Read Charge Rates screen.

4. Highlight the block of time for which you wish to assign a charge rate by pressing the Mark key (press F1 twice to verify the Mark key on your computer) and using your right cursor arrow to highlight the entire line. Then use your down cursor arrow until you have blocked the entire screen and press Enter. You see the Select Charge Rate menu.

5. Highlight Other Charge Rate and press Enter. You now see the New Charge Rate Screen. Leave Multiplier set to 1 and Divisor set to 1.

6. Press Esc twice and then press Enter.

Do the same for each service for which you will be charging.

After the period of time you have chosen as your monitoring period, use Atotal (see "Accounting Reports" at the beginning of this chapter) to determine the total use for each service.

HOW TO CALCULATE CHARGE RATES

Assume you want to charge $200 per week for blocks read. You have monitored the total use for this service and you know that 40,000 blocks are being read each week. You have to determine the monetary value of one charge. If we assume that one charge is 1 cent, we multiply the $200 charge by 100, giving us a figure of 20,000. Now we use this formula: multiplier (amount charged for blocks read)/divisor (total use). In our example, the charge rate is as follows:

$$20,000(\text{multiplier})/40,000(\text{divisor}) = .5 \text{ or } 1/2.$$

HOW TO CHANGE CHARGE RATES

To change the charge rates to 1/2, do the following:

1. Type SYSCON and press Enter at the DOS prompt. You are in the Available Topics menu.

2. Highlight Accounting and press Enter. You are now in the Accounting menu.

3. Highlight Blocks Read Charge Rates and press Enter. You see the Blocks Read Charge Rates screen.

4. Highlight the block of time for which you wish to assign a charge rate by pressing the Mark key (press F1 twice to verify the Mark key on your computer) and using your right cursor arrow to highlight the entire line. Then use your down cursor arrow until you have blocked the entire screen and press Enter. You see the Select Charge Rate menu.

5. Highlight Other Charge Rate and press Enter. You now see the New Charge Rate Screen. Leave Multiplier set to 1 and Divisor set to 2.

6. Press Esc twice and then press Enter.

Calculate the correct charge rate and make the change for each charged service following the steps outlined above.

ACCOUNT BALANCES

You (the supervisor) can assign account balances to users that will determine how much usage they have for each service. You can also assign them credit for each service. You can assign a default account balance for all users or you can assign individual account balances by user. These account balances can be changed by you, but the users who have been changed must log out and then back in before the changes will take effect.

NOTE: If a user is told by the system to log out because their account balance is too low, they must log out. If they do not, the file server will log them out and they will lose all data that has not been saved.

How to Set Up Default (System) Account Balances

Default account balances are automatically assigned to any user created after the default account balance is set up. To set up a default account balance do the following:

1. Type SYSCON Enter at the DOS prompt. You are in the Available Topics menu.

2. Highlight Supervisor Options and press Enter. You now see the Supervisor Options menu.

3. Highlight Default Account Balance/Restrictions and press Enter. You are now in the Default Account Balance/Restrictions screen.

4. If you want this account to have an expiration date, highlight Account Has Expiration Date, type Y and press Enter. You will then be asked for an expiration date. Type in the date of expiration and press Enter.

5. Highlight Account Balance and type the account balance you want the users to have. Each time a service is charged to a user, the account balance will be lower. Account balances are assigned in charges; for example, an account balance of 500 gives the user 500 charges. The default is 0.

6. If you want to assign unlimited credit to this account balance, highlight Allow Unlimited Credit, type Y, and press Enter.

7. If you want to allow limited credit, leave the Allow Unlimited Credit option set to no and highlight Low Balance Limit. Enter the amount of credit you want to assign to each user.

If you enter a negative number you allow a user to exceed his account balance by that amount before he can no longer receive services. For example, if you entered −50 in the Low Balance Limit option, when a user's account dropped to 0, they would still be able to receive services for 50 more charges.

8. When all of the account balance options have been entered, press Esc to exit the menu.

How to Set Up Individual User Account Balances

1. Type SYSCON Enter at the DOS prompt. You are in the Available Topics menu.

2. Highlight User Information and press Enter. You are in the User Names screen.

3. Highlight the user you want to assign an account balance and press Enter. The User Information menu appears.

4. Highlight Account Balance and press Enter. You are now in the Account Balance For User screen.

5. Highlight Account Balance and type the account balance you want the users to have. Each time a service is charged to a user, the account balance will be lower. Account balances are assigned in charges, for example an account balance of 500 gives the user 500 charges. The default is 0.

6. If you want to assign unlimited credit to this account balance, highlight Allow Unlimited Credit, type Y, and press Enter.

7. If you want to allow limited credit, leave the Allow Unlimited Credit option set to no and highlight Low Balance Limit. Enter the amount of credit you want to assign to each user.

   If you enter a negative number, you allow a user to exceed his account balance by that amount before he can no longer receive services. For example, if you entered −50 in the Low Balance Limit option, when a user's account dropped to 0, they would still be able to receive services for 50 more charges.

8. When all of the account balance options have been entered press Esc to exit the menu.

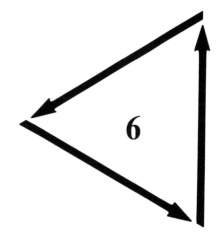

6

Menu Utility

NOVELL'S Menu Utility is a feature that allows you to create customized menus to access programs and other applications used on the network. NetWare comes with a default Main Menu that allows users to access other Novell menu utilities without using the DOS command line. The real strength of this utility lies in the fact that additional menus and submenus can be created that allow every user to access their applications through menus customized for them.

WHY USE MENUS?

Although any feature or application accessed through a menu can also be accessed through the DOS command line, there are excellent reasons for using menus.

- Menus make NetWare almost completely transparent for the end user. The user does not have to memorize or type the commands necessary to run applications through the network. With the commands incorporated into a menu, just by making a menu selection, a user can properly execute and use the selected application.

- Menus can be customized for different users to accommodate their level of expertise and their application use.

- Menus save a great deal of time by combining many steps into one menu selection.

- More experienced users can use or bypass menus at need.

SOME GENERAL INFORMATION ABOUT THE MENU UTILITY

Before creating your menus, check the following:

1. The following files must be loaded into the SYS:PUBLIC directory (this should have been done during the installation process):

SYS$MSG.DAT	MENUPARZ.HLP
SYS$ERR.DAT	MENU.EXE
IBM$RUN.OVL	MENUPARZ.EXE
SYS$HELP.DAT	

2. You should also map a search drive to the directory which contains COMMAND.COM. It should be in your DOS directory. See Chapter 4 for search drive mapping information.

3. All of the directories being accessed by the menus should be created and the necessary software installed.

4. Novell menus are created as ASCII text files. You need a text editor to make the menus. Usually, the menus are created in the DOS EDLIN program or in a word processor, such as WordPerfect, that allows you to save the file in an ASCII format.

The Novell menu program automatically alphabetizes your menu options. So, no matter what order you enter the menu options, they always appear alphabetically on the screen.

We have created a menu for Bob, the owner of ABC Paper Company. When Bob logs on to the network, the menu in Fig. 6-1 appears on the screen.

HOW TO MAKE A USER MENU

For purposes of organization, we have also created several submenus for Bob. When he highlights WordPerfect and presses Enter, he goes into

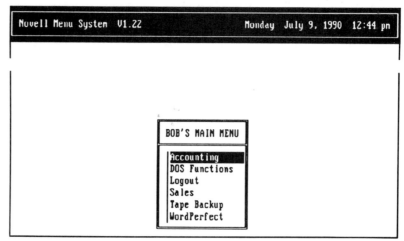

Fig. 6-1. The menu Bob accesses upon logging on to the network

the WordPerfect submenu. The same submenu system is used for the DOS Functions, Sales, and Accounting options. Figures 6-2 through 6-5 show the submenus.

Bob's Main Menu Text File

Figure 6-6 shows the text file we create that, when Novell's menu utility is being used, becomes Bob's menu. Each line of this text file is completed by pressing Enter.

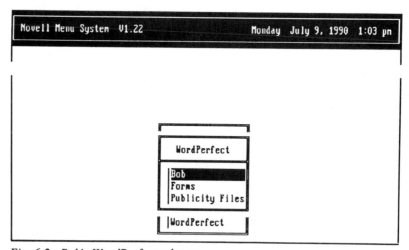

Fig. 6-2. Bob's WordPerfect submenu

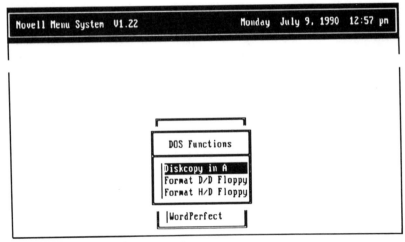

Fig. 6-3. Bob's DOS functions submenu

The following paragraphs explain the various commands in the text file used to create Bob's menu. In some cases, we have explained single lines. In other cases, we have explained groups of lines that make up a complete routine.

%BOB'S MAIN MENU   The first line of Bob's menu is the title of the menu. This must be typed at the left margin. All menu titles and menu options must be entered at the left margin. Spaces before text indicate that

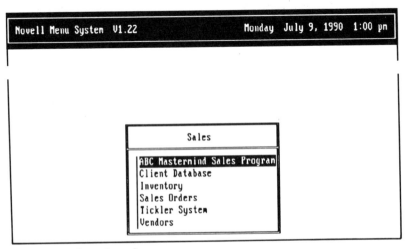

Fig. 6-4. Bob's sales submenu

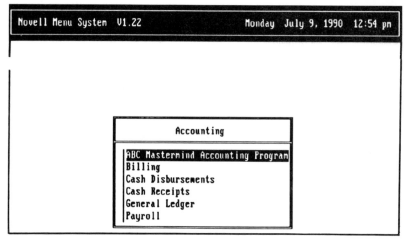

Fig. 6-5. Bob's accounting submenu

```
%BOB'S MAIN MENU
WordPerfect
  %WordPerfect
Sales
  %Sales
Accounting
  %Accounting
DOS Functions
  %DOS Functions
Logout
  !logout
Tape Backup
  echo off
  cls
  h:
  cd\
  cd\tape
  tape
%WordPerfect
Publicity Files
  echo off
  cls
  map p:=server_1/sys:publicit
  p:
  wp
```
Fig. 6-6. Bob's main menu text file

Fig. 6-6. Continued.

```
Bob
  echo off
  cls
  j:
  wp
Forms
  echo off
  cls
  map m:=server_1/sys:forms
  m:
  wp
%Sales
Inventory
  echo off
  cls
  capture ll p0 nb nff ti=5
  map n:=server_1/sys2:db/material
  n:
  inv
ABC Mastermind Sales Program
  echo off
  cls
  capture ll p0 nb nff ti=5
  w:
  abcmm
Vendors
  echo off
  cls
  capture ll p0 nb nff ti=5
  map o:=server_1/sys2:db/material
  o:
  ven
Client Database
  echo off
  cls
  capture ll p0 nb nff ti=5
  i:
  clients
Sales Orders
  echo off
  cls
  capture ll p0 nb nff ti=5
  map s:=server_1/sys2:db/sales
  s:
  orders
Tickler System
  echo off
  cls
```

```
          capture ll p0 nb nff ti=5
          map t:=server_1/sys2:db/tickler
          t:
          tickler
%Accounting
ABC Mastermind Accounting Program
          echo off
          cls
          capture ll p1 nb nff ti=5
          v:
          abcacc
Cash Receipts
          echo off
          cls
          capture ll p1 nb nff ti=5
          map r:=server_1/sys3:paydata
          r:
          receipts
Cash Disbursements
          echo off
          cls
          capture ll p2 nb nff ti=5
          map k:=server_1/sys3:paydata
          k:
          disburse
General Ledger
          echo off
          cls
          capture ll p1 nb nff ti=5
          map q:=server_1/sys3:gl
          q:
          gl
Payroll
          echo off
          cls
          capture ll p2 nb nff ti=5
          map r:=server_1/sys3:gl
          r:
          payroll
Billing
          echo off
          cls
          capture ll p1 nb nff ti=5
          map s:=server_1/sys3:orders
          s:
          billing
%DOS Functions
```

```
Format H/D Floppy
   echo off
   cls
   format a:
Format D/D Floppy
   echo off
   cls
   format a:/4
Diskcopy in A
   echo off
   cls
   diskcopy a: a:
```

Fig. 6-6. Ends.

a command follows. We have used uppercase letters. You may choose to use either upper or lowercase letters or any combination of the two. The menu will appear exactly as you type it. The % sign indicates that a menu name follows.

You can also specify the position of the menu on the screen and the menu color. These options are explained in detail later in this chapter.

WordPerfect   The second line in the text file indicates the menu option WordPerfect. This must be typed exactly as you want it to appear on the menu.

%WordPerfect   This line is indented two or three spaces to indicate that a command will follow. The % sign tells the menu program to go to the line starting with %WordPerfect. When Bob selects WordPerfect on the main menu, he will activate a submenu entitled WordPerfect.

Sales   The fourth line in our text file, Sales, is at the left margin. This indicates that it is a main menu option.

%Sales   This line, indented two spaces, tells the menu program that a command is to follow. The % sign tells the Menu program to go to the matching submenu title. When Bob selects Sales on his main menu, the submenu Sales appears on the screen.

Accounting and DOS Function Options   These entries perform the same function as previous four entries.

Accounting
   %Accounting

DOS Functions
%DOS Functions

The explanation given in the previous line applies to these entries also.

The Logout Menu Option Lines   This option automatically logs Bob off the network

Logout
 !Logout

!Logout is indented two spaces to tell the menu program that a command follows. !Logout is the command used to exit the menu and log out of the network. The !Logout command closes all files that have been opened by the menu program. The ! must precede Logout. Otherwise, you will get error messages when you select Logout.

The Tape Backup Main Menu Option   We have reproduced the entire Tape Backup option routine here. The indented section below Tape Backup is a series of DOS commands. Together, they make up a short batch file. Each command is discussed in the following paragraphs. Tape Backup must be typed at the left margin. This indicates it is a menu option.

Tape Backup
 echo off
 cls
 h:
 cd\
 cd\tape
 tape

Echo off is indented two spaces. It is a DOS command that prevents the commands in the rest of this routine from printing on the screen. For more information on echo off, refer to your DOS manual.

Cls is indented two spaces. It is a DOS command that clears the screen of any text. For more information on cls refer to your DOS manual.

H: is also indented two spaces, indicating to the menu program that it is a command. Because H: is mapped to SYS3: in Bob's login script (refer to Chapter 4, "Login Scripts" for detailed explanations on mapping) H: takes Bob to SYS3:.

Cd\ is indented two spaces. It is a DOS command that changes the current directory to the root directory of SYS3:. For more information on cd\, refer to your DOS manual.

Cd\tape is indented two spaces. It is a DOS command that changes the directory from SYS3:\ to SYS3:TAPE (for more information refer to your DOS manual).

Tape is indented two spaces and is the execute command for the tape backup program.

When Bob highlights Tape Backup on his main menu and presses Enter, each of the preceding commands will execute in the order in which they were typed and Bob will have accessed his tape backup program.

This menu subroutine uses the DOS command, cd, to change directories.

The WordPerfect Submenu   When WordPerfect is selected from Bob's menu, the WordPerfect submenu appears on the screen. See Fig. 6-2. The following subroutine creates the Publicity Files option. It also contains the code to execute WordPerfect from the PUBLICIT directory. The following subroutine was done by mapping a drive to a specific directory (for more detailed information on mapping drives, refer to Chapter 4, "Login Scripts").

```
%WordPerfect
Publicity Files
    echo off
    cls
    map p:=server_1/sys:publicit
    p:
    wp
```

%WordPerfect is the submenu title of the WordPerfect submenu. It is at the left margin and must exactly match the submenu option you typed earlier (%WordPerfect at line 3). Once again, you have the option of adding qualifiers to indicate the position of the submenu on your screen and to specify colors. These qualifiers are discussed later in this chapter.

Publicity Files is the first option in the WordPerfect submenu. It is typed at the left margin and will appear in the submenu as a menu option exactly as it is typed.

Echo off and cls are DOS commands explained in the previous Tape Backup section.

Map p:=server_1/sys:publicit maps drive P: to the file server named SERVER_1, the volume named SYS: and the directory named PUB-LICIT. (For more detailed information concerning drive mapping, refer to Chapter 4, "Login Scripts".)

P: changes directory to P: and brings Bob to the PUBLICIT directory on SERVER_1/SYS:.

Wp is the command to execute WordPerfect. Because WordPerfect is mapped to a search drive the program can be executed from within the publicit directory. For more information concerning search drives, refer to Chapter 4, "Login Scripts".

When Bob highlights Publicity Files in the WordPerfect submenu, he starts WordPerfect. His default directory, while in this option, is PUBLICIT.

WordPerfect Submenu—Bob Option   Bob is the next option in the WordPerfect submenu. It is typed at the left margin and appears in the submenu exactly as it is typed.

```
Bob
   echo off
   cls
   j:
   wp
```

Echo off and cls are DOS commands. They are explained in the previous Tape Back section.

J: is mapped to Bob's user directory in his login script (for more information on login scripts, refer to Chapter 4, "Login Scripts") and brings him to that directory.

The last line, wp, executes WordPerfect from within Bob's user directory.

The Forms Submenu Option   The following subroutine places the Forms option in the WordPerfect submenu. It also supplies the commands to execute WordPerfect while in the FORMS directory. Its operation is similar to the preceding sections.

```
Forms
   echo off
   cls
   map m:=server_1/sys:forms
   m:
   wp
```

Remember, the Novell menu utility automatically alphabetizes your menu options. Therefore, even though we typed Publicity Files first, Bob second, and Forms third, the submenu will list them in this order: Bob, Forms, Publicity Files.

The Inventory Option of the Sales Submenu   Figure 6-4 shows the next submenu, Sales. It offers Bob a choice of options. He can go to the ABC Mastermind Sales Program screen and access all of the options of the ABC sales program, or he can access certain portions of the sales program directly from the Sales submenu without having to go through the ABC Mastermind Sales Program screen. This keeps the number of screens Bob uses to access the information he normally needs to a minimum. The description of the submenu heading and the Inventory option follows.

```
%Sales
Inventory
    echo off
    cls
    capture l1 p0 nb nff ti=5
    map n:=server_1/sys2:db/material
    n:
    inv
```

%Sales is the title of the Sales submenu. It is typed at the left margin and must exactly match the submenu option you specified earlier in the main menu (line 5, %Sales). The title appears exactly as typed.

Inventory is an option in the Sales submenu.

Echo off and cls are DOS commands discussed in previous Tape Backup sections.

Capture l1 p0 nb nff ti=5 is a printer capture command that reroutes the local printer LPT1 to the network printer 0. It specifies no banner, no form feed, and a timeout of 5. For more detailed information on the CAPTURE command and its qualifying flags, refer to Chapter 7, "Printers."

Map n:=server_1/sys2:db/material maps the drive N: to the file server named SERVER_1, the volume named SYS2:, the directory named db, and the subdirectory named material. (For more information on drive mapping, refer to Chapter 4, "Login Scripts.")

N: changes directory to the mapped drive N.

Inv executes the inventory portion of the sales program.

ABC Mastermind Sales Program Option   The Mastermind Sales Program is another option in Bob's Sales submenu. The list of commands shown here creates this option. An explanation of how it works follows.

```
ABC Mastermind Sales Program
  echo off
  cls
  capture 11 p0 nb nff ti=5
  w:
  abcmm
```

ABC Mastermind Sales Program is an option in the Sales submenu. The text in the submenu appears exactly as typed.

Echo off and cls are DOS commands that are discussed in the preceding section on the Tape Backup option.

Capture 11 p0 nb nff ti=5 is a printer command that reroutes the local printer LPT1 to the network printer designated as 0. It specifies no banner, no form feed, and a timeout of 5. (For more information concerning the CAPTURE command, refer to Chapter 7, "Printers.")

W: is the designation of a search drive in the login script. It maps the path SERVER_1/SYS2:DB to drive W:. For more information concerning search drives, refer to Chapter 4, "Login Scripts."

Abcmm is the execute command for the ABC Mastermind Sales Program.

The rest of Bob's menu was created following the steps outlined above. We typed the rest of the Sales submenu options, the Accounting submenu and its options, and the DOS Functions submenu and its options.

Reusing Mapped Drive Designations

You can reuse a mapped drive designation. For example, you can map Inventory to N:=SERVER_1/SYS2:DB/MATERIAL and also map Cash Receipts to N:=SERVER_1/SYS3:PAYDATA in your text file. When you highlight Inventory and press Enter, n: is mapped to SERVER_1/SYS2:DB/MATERIAL. When you highlight Cash Receipts and press Enter, however, N: is remapped to SERVER_1/SYS3:PAYDATA. As explained above, when a path is remapped to an existing drive map, the old map is overwritten with the new one. See Chapter 4 for further information on drive mapping.

Save the Text File

Save the file in an ASCII format in your SYS:PUBLIC directory. Refer to either your DOS manual, if you used EDLIN, or to your word processor manual on how to save. Remember, you are limited to eight letters plus a three letter extension for your file name. We named our file

Bob.mnu. The .MNU extension informs the Novell menu utility that this file is a menu.

Accessing Your Menu in DOS

Because you saved the text file in the SYS:PUBLIC directory (which is mapped to a search drive), you can access the menu from anywhere in DOS by typing the following:

MENU BOB Enter

MENU always precedes the name of the text file. If your text file has an .MNU extension, you do not need to type the extension. However, if it has any other extension, it must be included in your DOS command. For example, if you had saved Bob's menu as BOB.MEN, you would have to type the following at the DOS prompt:

MENU BOB.MEN Enter

Commands typed at the DOS prompt are not case sensitive.

Accessing Your Menu from a Login Script

When Bob logs on to the network, we want him to automatically access his main menu. To do this, we must modify Bob's Login Script as follows:

1. Type SYSCON Enter at the DOS prompt.

2. Highlight User Information and press Enter. You are in the User Names list.

3. Highlight Bob and press Enter. You have accessed the User Information screen.

4. Highlight Login Script and press Enter. Bob's user login script appears.

5. Bring your cursor down past the last line of text and type

EXIT "MENU BOB" Enter

This must be the last entry in the login script. For more information on login scripts, refer to Chapter 4, "Login Scripts."

USING VARIABLES IN YOUR MENU

It is possible for users to input variable information while in a menu. This can automate many DOS functions such a directory lists, file copying, or viewing a DOS directory. It is done by assigning a variable to a value entered by the user. For example, to view the contents of a drive or directory in your menu text file:

DIR
    dir @1"Enter Drive or Directory You Wish to View"

DIR is the option that appears on your menu.

Dir is the DOS command to list the contents of a directory. @1 represents variable 1 and displays the message Enter Drive or Directory You Wish to View. The quotation marks indicate the text that is to appear on the screen. They are not displayed. When the user enters the drive or directory he or she wishes to view, variable 1 is replaced by that choice. For instance, if the user typed F: at the Enter Drive or Directory You Wish to View prompt, he or she would then get a listing of the contents of F:.

Each new DOS command supercedes the previous, and any variables included with it should start with a value of 1.

HOW TO CONTROL THE PLACEMENT OF MENUS ON THE SCREEN

The Novell default places all menus and submenus at the center of the screen. You can override this default and specify the location of your menus and submenus on the screen with location values to indicate vertical and horizontal placement.

Vertical Placement

Vertical placement is measured in lines. To determine vertical placement, you need to decide how many lines from the top of the screen you want the menu to be and how many lines the menu itself occupies. For example, Bob's Main Menu occupies 7 lines. We want the menu to appear at line 6 on the screen. We need to use the following equation:

$$6 + 7/2 = 9.5$$

where 6 indicates the number of lines from the top of the screen and 7/2 indicates the number of lines the menu occupies divided by 2. The result,

9.5 is the vertical placement value. If we wanted Bob's menu to appear 6 lines down on the screen we would replace %BOB'S MAIN MENU with the following in the BOB.MNU text file:

%BOB'S MAIN MENU, 9.5,,

with 9.5 representing vertical placement and the commas that follow representing the defaults for horizontal placement and the color palette. These options are separated by commas when there is a value for each. When the value is the default, a comma with no value will so indicate.

Horizontal Placement

Horizontal placement is measured in columns (with a column being a character or space). To determine where on the screen your menu should be placed, first decide how many columns from the left you want your menu to be and then determine how many columns your menu occupies. We know Bob's menu is 15 columns wide (13 characters plus two spaces). To place the menu BOB.MNU 6 columns from the left, we would use the following formula:

$$6 + 15/2 = 13.5$$

where 6 represents the number of columns from the left we want the menu to be placed and 15/2 represents the number of columns in the menu divided by 2. The answer, 13.5, is the value of our horizontal placement. If we wanted Bob's menu to be 6 lines down and 6 columns from the left of the screen, we would replace %BOB'S MAIN MENU in our BOB.MNU text file with the following:

%BOB'S MAIN MENU, 9.5,13.5,

with 9.5 representing the vertical placement, 13.5 representing the horizontal placement. The last comma, with no following value, represents the default color palette.

Entering %BOB'S MAIN MENU with no value specification assumes the Novell defaults. If any value is used (vertical placement, horizontal placement, or color palette), commas must be used between the menu title and each of the three variables. A missing placement variable is shown by two commas with no space between them. A missing color palette is shown by the final comma without any following variable.

CHANGING THE COLORS OF YOUR MENUS

You may change the colors of your menus (including the Novell utility menus) by using the Novell utility Colorpal. The color table used by Colorpal is located in the IBM$RUN.OVL file in the SYS:PUBLIC directory. If you run Colorpal from the SYS:PUBLIC, you will change the system default for all color monitors on the network. Therefore, if you wish to change colors for your computer only, you will have to create new color palettes from a directory other than SYS:PUBLIC.

Creating a Color Palette

1. If you do not wish to change the system defaults, copy IBM$RUN.OVL from the SYS:PUBLIC directory to another directory or run Colorpal from a directory other than SYS:PUBLIC.

2. Map the drive in which you create a new palette as your first search drive. Refer to Chapter 4 for more information on drive mapping.

3. Type COLORPAL Enter. You now see the Defined Palettes menu.

4. Palettes 0 through 4 are already in use by Novell. To add palette 5, press Enter. You see a list of defined palettes numbered from 0 to 5.

5. Highlight the palette you wish to edit and press Enter. You are in the Edit Attribute menu. The attributes you can change are as follows:

ATTRIBUTE	DESCRIPTION
Background Normal	The color used for the background on which the menu titles and text are displayed.
Foreground Normal	The color used for regular text and border displays.
Foreground Intense	The color used to highlight the text and borders for selected menu options.
Foreground Reverse	The color used for the text in the highlight bar.
Background Reverse	The color used for the highlight bar.

6. Highlight the attribute you wish to change and press Enter. You will see the Select Colors screen. If you are changing a foreground color, you have these choices:

Black	Light Cyan
Blue	Light Green
Brown	Light Magenta
Cyan	Light Red
Dark Gray	Magenta
Green	Red
Intense White	White
Light Blue	Yellow

If you are changing the background color, you have one of these choices:

Black	Green
Blue	Magenta
Brown	Red
Cyan	White

7. Highlight the new color you want to use and press Enter. Repeat steps 4 through 7 until you have made all the changes you want.

8. Press Esc until you come to the Save Changes confirmation screen.

9. Highlight Yes and press Enter. You will be asked to confirm that you want to exit Colorpal.

10. Highlight Yes and press Enter.

NOTE: To modify the IBM$RUN.OVL file you must have read, write, open and delete rights.

Deleting a Color Palette

1. Type COLORPAL Enter in the directory in which the palette was created. You will see the Defined Palettes menu.

2. Highlight the palette you are deleting and press Delete. The Delete Palette confirmation screen appears. Remember, color palettes 0 through 4 are used by Novell and cannot be deleted.

3. Highlight Yes and press Enter.

Using Color Palettes in Your Menu

Assume that you have just created palette 5 (remember palettes 0 through 4 are already being used as default Novell colors). You wish to use this new palette in Bob's main menu. You would change the title line of BOB.MNU from %BOB'S MAIN MENU to look like this:

%BOB'S MAIN MENU,,,5

where the first comma indicates qualifiers will follow, the second and third commas indicate default vertical and horizontal placement, and the number 5 indicates the menu's color palette.

Color Palettes for Non-IBM Type Computers

If you have a computer with a monochrome monitor that runs from a composite color adapter (such at a Compaq or an AT&T 6300), your default screen values will render the text illegible. You can solve this problem by doing any one of the following:

- Change the short machine type in the SHELL.CFG file on your boot disk to CMPQ.

- Change the prefix of the CMPQ$RUN.OVL file found in the SYS:PUBLIC to match the short machine type in the SHELL.CFG file.

- Change the default color palettes to black or white using Colorpal.

ERROR MESSAGES RELATING TO MENUS

If your menu does not run, you will probably receive at least one error message. The most common messages are listed below with their explanations.

1. *Program execution should continue normally.*

   This message indicates that there is something wrong with your text file, but that the menu is able to run.

2. *The current operation cannot be completed.*

This message indicates that you have selected an option that cannot be accessed. Check your drive mapping and the name of the file you are executing to be sure they are correct. Verify that you have trustee rights to access the option. Drive mapping is discussed in Chapter 4. Chapter 3 covers trustee rights.

3. *Further program execution is not possible.*

This Fatal Error message indicates that the Novell menu program cannot run your menu. Check to be sure you have saved the text file in an ASCII format.

4. *No commands for menu option.*

This message indicates that you have a menu option with no commands. Check your text file to be sure you included a start-up command with the option.

5. *No options for menu.*

This message indicates that a main menu or submenu was created but no options were included.

6. *Process new menu not on menu line.*

This message indicates that the % sign was left out on a submenu title.

7. *Unable to find menu header.*

This message indicates that the Novell menu program was unable to find the % sign at the beginning of the main menu title. The Novell menu program does not recognize a menu as valid without the % sign.

8. *Unable to get next option.*

This message indicates that the menu program is unable to read an option. Check your text file to be sure that nothing has been deleted from the menu script for that option.

9. *Unable to scan menu title.*

This message indicates that the Novell menu program could not scan the menu title. Check to be certain that you have text following the % sign in your text file.

10. *Unable to seek on menu file.*
         and
    Unable to seek on restart file.

    These messages indicate a problem with your hard drive. Back up your data immediately!

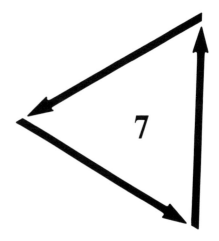

Printers

INDEPENDENT PC's are usually connected to a single printer which is used only by that particular computer. While hardware devices can be purchased to allow more than one user to access a printer, it is inefficient and expensive to attempt to connect several computers to more than one printer on a non-networked system. One of the principal advantages of networking is the ability to share printers efficiently through the use of the networking software. This is accomplished through a process called spooling.

CONCEPTS OF PRINTER SHARING

When printers are properly spooled, each terminal on the network is connected to every printer attached to the network. A user will send a job to the printer of choice, usually using application software to do so. It is then up to Novell to receive the print job and direct it to the correct printer.

When several users are sending print jobs, it is necessary for Novell to properly queue the jobs so that they are printed in an orderly fashion and traffic jams do not ensue. In addition, provision must be made for users (queue managers) to intervene in the event that a job must be redirected or the order of the queue changed. To provide for this intervention, it is necessary for a queue manager to monitor the path of a print job from its inception to its completion and to be able to intercede at any point in the process.

The process of printing a job through a network, therefore, is a very complex one. Not only must Novell interpret all instructions sent by the applications software, it must also direct all jobs to the correct printers and organize the flow of print jobs at every level. The capacity for errors or problems is immense.

Some application software has excellent printer drivers (communications programs between application and printers). Other software is capable of sending only primitive instructions to Novell and the printers. When application software falls down on the job, the supervisor must compensate by adding the necessary instructions to enable Novell to properly accomplish the task. For example, the supervisor can use PRINTDEF to define print devices (such as printers or plotters) and set up print functions (such as orientation and typeface). In addition, the supervisor can use command line utilities such as CAPTURE to direct a job to a specific printer.

Errors can also occur in the process of queuing. Again, the supervisor or console operator must intervene and correct the problem.

WHAT IS A PRINT QUEUE?

A network print queue is a holding area that receives multiple print jobs, organizes them, and prints them in the order they were received. A queue manager can add to, delete from, or rearrange the print order of jobs in a queue. It is possible to have several queues connected to one printer. The supervisor would then be able to set the priority of all of the queues attached to a printer. For example, printer 0 might have three queues attached to it: sales, word processing, and accounting. The supervisor can then determine that the jobs should be printed in the following order: first all word processing jobs can be printed, then sales, and, last in order of priority, accounting. In addition, the queue manager can also determine the order of priority within the manager's own queue, i.e., word processing. It is also possible to have several printers connected to one queue. In this way jobs within a particular queue could be sent to any printer attached to that queue, thus speeding up the printing.

This chapter covers the print features in Novell necessary to regulate the complex operation of overseeing a print job from beginning to end.

VAPs

NetWare can only accommodate five printers, three parallel and two serial. Very large LANs often require more than five printers and often the printers have to be spread over a large distance far removed from the file server. Netware v2.1 and above supports remote workstation servers known as VAPs (VALUE-ADDED Process). VAPs are provided through third-party software manufacturers. Each VAP is installed and operated according to its own instructions. There are many such programs on the market today. We strongly recommend Queue It by Brightwork Development, because of the excellent results our larger clients have had with it. It would be impossible in this book to describe each VAP on the market and how each one operates. Supervisors using VAPs should refer to the documentation included with each package.

PRINTDEF

Most software packages on the market today come with fairly sophisticated printer drivers that allow you to choose and modify printer applications, eliminating the need for any additional instructions by Novell. However, if your applications software is too primitive to allow you to set up and identify print devices, functions, and forms, you will have to do so through Novell using the PRINTDEF feature. This feature allows supervisors to define print devices (printers and plotters), set up functions using escape sequences, set modes that combine a sequence of functions, and set up forms that define the size of paper being used.

Novell comes with 30 predefined print devices. (See Table 7-1.) If you can use one of these predefined files, you can save a great deal of time.

Setting Up Print Device Definitions

For Novell to use these print device definitions, the supervisor must copy them into the Printdef menu. To access Printdef from the DOS prompt, type PRINTDEF. The menu in Fig. 7-1 appears:

1. Highlight Print Devices and press Enter.

2. In the Print Device Options, Fig. 7-2, menu, highlight Import Print Device and press Enter. You have accessed the Source Directory box. It shows your current directory.

Table 7-1. Novell NetWare Supported
Print Devices

Filename	Printer
APPIMAGE.PDF	Apple Imagewriter II
APPLASER.PDF	Apple Laserwriter I/PLUS
CIT120D.PDF	Citizen 120-D
CIT20.PDF	Citizen 20
CIT224.PDF	Citizen 224
CITOH310.PDF	CITOH 310/315
CTOH600.PDF	CITOH 600
DIAB630.PDF	Diablo 630
EPEX80.PDF	Epson FX80/FX100
EPEX800.PDF	Epson EX-800
EPEX86.PDF	Epson FX86E/FX286E
EPLD2500.PDF	Epson LD-2500
EPLQ800.PDF	Epson LQ-800/LQ-1000
EPLX80.PDF	Epson LX-80
EPLX800.PDF	Epson LX-800
HPLASER.PDF	Hewlett-Packard Laserjet I/II
IBM4201.PDF	IBM Proprinter 4201
IBMPRO2.PDF	IBM Proprinter II/XL
NEC2050.PDF	NEC Spinwriter 2050/3050
NEC8810.PDF	NEC Spinwriter 8810/8830
NECP6.PDF	NEC Pinwriter P-6
OKI192.PDF	Okidata Microline 192/193
OKI290.PDF	Okidata 290
OKI390.PDF	Okidata 390
OKILASER.PDF	Okidata Laserline 6
PAN1080.PDF	Panasonic 1080/1080i
PAN1091.PDF	Panasonic 1091/1091i
STAR1000.PDF	Star NX-1000
STAR10X.PDF	Star Gemini 10X
TOSHP321.PDF	Toshiba P321

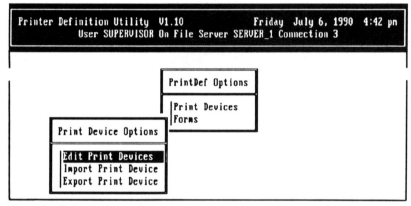

Fig. 7-1. *Printdef main menu*

Fig. 7-2. *Print device options menu*

3. If your current directory is not SYS:PUBLIC, use the Backspace key to delete the current directory. Now replace it with SYS: PUBLIC and press Enter. You are now in the Available .PDFs menu.

4. Highlight the .PDF file you want to copy and press Enter. You are returned to the Print Device Options menu.

5. If you do not wish to add any more print device definitions, press Esc to Exit to the PRINTDEF confirmation box, highlight Yes and press Enter.

6. Highlight Save Data Base, then Exit and press Enter.

If you wish to add a print device that is not included in the preceding list, you need to do the following from the Printdef Options menu:

1. Highlight Print Devices and press Enter. You have accessed the Print Device Options menu shown in Fig. 7-2.

2. Highlight Edit Print Devices and press Enter. You will see a list of Defined Print Devices. Press Insert to access the New Device Name screen.

3. Type the name of the print device you wish to add using up to eight characters. You may not use an extension and you may not use spaces. Then press Enter. You have been returned to the Defined Print Devices menu.

4. Highlight the print device you have entered and press Enter. You are in the Edit Device Options menu.

5. Highlight Device Functions and press Enter. You have accessed the Device Functions screen, with the word "Device" replaced by the name of the print device you have added. See Fig. 7-3 for an example of this screen.

6. Press Insert. You have accessed the Function Definition Form screen. Enter the name you wish to use to identify the printer

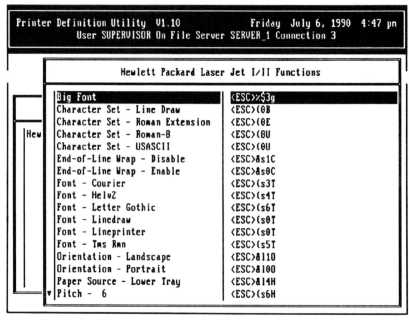

Fig. 7-3. Device functions screen for Hewlett Packard Laserjet I/II

function (i.e., reset, portrait, etc.) and press Enter. You are at the Escape Sequence screen.

NOTE: Always include the printer reset escape sequence.

7. Enter the actual escape sequence needed to perform the function you have just identified and press Enter. Printer escape sequences are found in the documentation accompanying the printer.

8. Press Esc and Enter to save the new escape sequence in the Device Functions list.

9. Repeat steps 5 through 8 for each function and escape sequence you are adding to a print device.

10. Press Esc to return to the Edit Device Options menu.

To edit any of the device functions:

1. Highlight the function you wish to edit and press Enter.

2. Backspace to delete the information you wish to change and type in the new function name or escape sequence.

3. Press Esc and Enter to save the changed function.

4. Press Esc to return to the Edit Device Options menu.

What Are Print Device Modes?

Print device modes are a combination of print device functions. Several print device functions can be combined into one print device mode that tells the printer how to print a specific job. For example, you could set up a print device mode called "Final" which combines the following functions: Reset, Orientation--Portrait, and 10cpi. To set up print device modes from the Printdef Options menu do the following:

1. Highlight Print Devices and press Enter. You are now in the Print Device Options menu.

2. Highlight Edit Device Options and press Enter. You are in the Defined Print Devices screen.

3. Highlight the print device you wish to assign a mode and press Enter. You are in the Edit Device Options screen.

4. Highlight Device Modes and press Enter. You are in the Device Modes screen. ("Device" will be replaced by the name of the printer you have selected.)

5. Highlight Re-initialize and press Enter. The Re-initialize Functions screen appears.

6. Press Insert and a list of all the functions which have been defined for the print device is displayed.

7. Highlight the escape sequence for resetting the print device and press Enter. If your printer needs more than one function to reset, use your Mark Key (press F1 twice to verify the Mark Key for your computer) to select all the needed functions. When you are finished marking, press Enter.

Once you have entered the Re-initialize mode functions, you can begin to create additional print device modes to suit your printing needs. From the Printdef Options menu:

1. Highlight Print Device and press Enter. You are in the Print Device Options menu.

2. Highlight Edit Print Devices and press Enter. You have accessed the Defined Print Devices menu.

3. Highlight the print device you wish to edit and press Enter to take you to the Edit Device Options menu.

4. Highlight Device Modes and press Enter. You are in the Device Modes screen. ("Device" is replaced by the name of the printer you have selected.) Press Insert. You now see the New Mode Name screen appear.

5. Type the name of the mode you are adding and press Enter. You are in the New Mode Name Functions screen. (New Mode Name has been replaced by the name of the mode you have added).

6. Press Insert to see a list of all functions that have been defined for the print device.

7. Highlight the function you wish to add to the mode and press Enter.

8. To add multiple functions to the mode, use your Mark key to highlight the functions you are adding and press Enter. (Press F1 twice to verify the Mark key for your computer).

9. To delete a function from the mode, highlight the function and press delete.

10. To delete more than one function from the mode, use your Mark key to highlight the functions you wish to delete and press delete. (Press F1 twice to verify the Mark key for your computer.)

11. Press Esc until you come to the Exit Options menu.

12. Highlight Save Data Base, then EXIT and press Enter.

COPYING PRINT DEVICE DEFINITIONS AND MODES BETWEEN FILE SERVERS

When your network has more than one file server, you sometimes have different print device definitions on each one. It is possible to copy these print device definitions between file servers rather than re-entering print device definitions and modes for both servers. To do this, you must have supervisor privileges on both file servers. If you have these privileges, you can export the print device definition by following these steps:

1. At the DOS prompt, type PRINTDEF and press Enter. You see the PrintDef Options menu.

2. Highlight Print Devices and press Enter. You have accessed the Print Device Options menu.

3. Highlight Export Print Device and press Enter. You see a list of Defined Print Devices.

4. Highlight the definition you wish to export and press Enter. The Destination Directory screen appears showing your current directory.

5. Use your Backspace key to delete the complete directory path and press Insert twice. You now see a list of all file servers attached to the network.

6. Highlight the file server you wish to export the file to and press Enter. If you are not attached to the file server you are exporting to, you are asked for your login name and password. Once attached to the file server, a menu listing the volumes of the destination file server is displayed.

7. Highlight the volume where you want the print device definition sent and press Enter. You now see a screen listing all of the directories in the selected volume.

8. Highlight the directory you want and press Enter. Continue selecting subdirectories until you have specified the complete path for the print device definition on the destination file server. Then press Esc and Enter. You see the Export File Name screen.

   Novell places all of its default print device definitions in the SYS:PUBLIC directory. We strongly suggest that you place any print device definitions you create in the same directory.

9. Type the name you are giving the print device definition. You can use up to eight characters in the name. You cannot use a file extension nor can you use spaces. Then press Enter.

10. Press Esc three times. When the Exit Printdef screen appears, highlight Yes and press Enter.

    Repeat these steps for each print device definition you wish to export.

Now that you have the print device file on your file server, preferably in the SYS:PUBLIC directory, you can copy it into Printdef for it to be used by Novell. At the DOS prompt, type PRINTDEF and press Enter.

1. Highlight Print Devices and press Enter.

2. In the Print Device Options menu, highlight Import Print Device and press Enter. You will have accessed the Source Directory screen showing your current directory.

3. If your current directory is not SYS:PUBLIC, use the Backspace key to delete the current directory. Type in SYS:PUBLIC and press Enter. You are now in the Available .PDFs menu.

4. Highlight the .PDF file you want to copy and press Enter. You are then returned to the Print Device Options menu.

5. If you are not going to add any more print device definitions, press Esc until you see the Exit Printdef confirmation box, highlight Yes and press Enter.

6. Highlight Save Data Base, then EXIT and press Enter.

Defining Forms

When you define a form in Printdef, you tell Novell the size of the paper you will be using. When this information is combined with print device definitions and modes in Printcon, the file server has a complete set of instructions on how to print a job. When you send a print job to the file server and specify a form, the server cannot print the job until that form is mounted. (For information on the Novell Mount command, see Chapter 9). To define a print form, do the following:

1. At the DOS prompt, type PRINTDEF and Enter. You are in the Printdef Options menu.

2. Highlight Forms and print Enter.

3. Press Insert and the Forms Definition Form screen appears. Type the name of the form you are adding and press Enter. The first character of the name must be a letter. The name cannot be longer than 12 characters. You cannot use spaces in the name. If you want a space, substitute an underscore (Shift-Hyphen, next to zero on most keyboards), for it.

4. Type the number of the form and press Enter. You may enter any number between zero and 255. Zero is the default form. Most supervisors assign zero to the most commonly used paper size.

5. Type the length of the form using lines per page and press Enter. You must have a number between 1 and 255. For example, if you are defining a form for an 8-1/2 by 11 inch paper size and your printer is set for 6 lines per inch, you would set the length of the form at 66 lines.

6. Type the width of the form in characters per line and press Enter. You must have a number between 1 and 999. Assume you are using 8-1/2 by 11 inch paper and your printer defaults to 10 characters per inch. The width of your form would be 85.

7. Press Esc and then answer Yes to confirm the changes.

8. To edit a form, highlight the form in the Forms list and press Enter. Move your cursor to the data in the form you wish to change and type in the new information. Press Esc and answer Yes to confirm the changes.

9. To delete a form, highlight the form you wish to delete in the Forms list and press delete. Highlight Yes and press Enter to confirm deletion.

10. To exit Printdef press Esc twice and you are in the Exit Printdef screen. Highlight Yes and press Enter. You have accessed the Exit Options menu. Highlight Save Data Base, then EXIT and press Enter.

PRINTCON

Once you have defined your devices, functions, modes and forms in Printdef you can use them to create print job configurations using the Printcon feature.

Setting Up Print Job Configurations

To set up a configuration to print invoices, you would follow these steps:

1. Type PRINTCON Enter at the DOS prompt. The Available Topics menu is displayed as shown in Fig. 7-4.

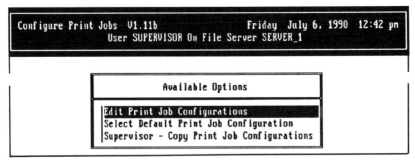

Fig. 7-4. Printcon main menu

2. Highlight Edit Print Job Configurations and press Enter. A list of existing print job configurations is displayed.

3. To add a new configuration to the list press Insert. The Enter New Name box will appear. Type in the name of the new configuration, in this case, INVOICE, and press Enter.

4. The Edit Print Job Configuration screen is displayed. See Fig. 7-5. This screen contains a number of parameters required to define and modify the configuration. See Table 7-2 for a list of these parameters and their definitions.

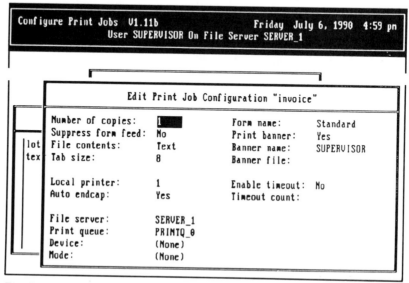

Fig. 7-5. *Screen used to edit print job configuration*

Table 7-2. **Edit Print Job Configuration Parameters**

Parameter	Description
Number of Copies	You can print from 1 to 65,000 copies of the job.
Suppress Form Feed	Entering Yes at this parameter instructs the printer not to feed a blank sheet of paper after each job is printed.
File Contents	There are two choices in File Contents—Text and Byte Stream. Text is used with ASCII text to instruct the print server to interpret all formatting commands. Byte-Stream is used when you print from an application (such as WordPerfect) and you want all the formatting commands handled by the application rather than the print server.

Table 7-2 Continued.

Parameter	*Description*
Tab Size	Used only if File Contents is set to Text. You can set your tabs from 1 to 18 spaces by entering the number of spaces in this field (the default is 8). All tabs in your file are then set to that number.
Form Name	You can use any of the forms defined in Printdef (the forms can be listed by striking any key while in this field).
Print Banner	Choose Yes or No. A banner is a printed sheet that precedes the job indicating the name of the print file and the person requesting the job. If you respond No, the banner is not printed.
Banner Name	The default banner name is your user login name. If you wish, you can type in a different banner name using up to 12 characters.
Banner File	The default is the name of the file. If you wish, you can type in a different file name (for the banner only) using up to 12 characters.
Local Printer	This is used only with the CAPTURE command (see "Printing from the Command Line" at the end of this chapter) to enter the Local Printer Port (lpt1; lpt2; or lpt3) the captured file is redirected from.
Auto Endcap	This is used only with the CAPTURE command (see "Printing from the Command Line" at the end of this chapter). It is usually used to reverse a NoAUTOENDCAP command (see "Printing from the Command Line" at the end of this chapter) or as an alternative to a TIMEOUT command (see TIMEOUT in "Printing from the Command Line" at the end of this chapter and Enable Timeout and Timeout Count below). If you answer Yes the print job is sent to the queue upon exiting an application. If you answer No the file will not be printed until you run ENDCAP.
Enable Timeout	This is used only with the CAPTURE command (see "Printing from the Command Line" at the end of this chapter). If you answer Yes the job you have

Table 7-2 Ends.

Parameter	Description
	captured is sent to the printer after the specified period of time (set in Timeout Count). If you answer No the job you have captured is sent to the printer according to the setting in the Auto endcap field. See "TIMEOUT" in "Printing from the Command Line" at the end of this chapter for more information about this feature.
Timeout Count	This determines the amount of time (in seconds) Novell waits before sending a file to queue. Enter a number from 1 to 1000 (the default is 5). 10 seconds is adequate for most applications. See "TIMEOUT" in "Printing from the Command Line" at the end of this chapter for more information about this feature.
File Server	Press any key to see a list of the file servers you can choose from, highlight the server you wish to use and press Enter.
Print Queue	Use this feature to choose the print queue to which the job is to be sent.
Device	Press any key to see a list of devices (printers or plotters) to choose from. Highlight your choice and press Enter. The Device you select must be connected to the queue selected in Print Queue, described above (see Chapter 9, "ADD QUEUE TO PRINTER" and Chapter 5, AUTOEXEC.SYS).
Mode	See the section in this chapter entitled "PRINTDEF" for information on how to set up modes. To list all modes available, press any key. Then highlight the mode you want to select and press Enter.

5. Edit this screen by using the arrow keys to highlight the field to be changed and press Enter. Type in the new value or select a value from the menu provided for that field, and press Enter to save the change.

6. When you have completed the print job configuration, press Escape.

7. To save your changes highlight Yes and press Enter.

Deleting a Print Job Configuration

Only supervisors or supervisor equivalents can delete print job configurations. The default print job configuration cannot be deleted. To delete a print job configuration follow these steps:

1. At the DOS prompt, type PRINTCON Enter. The Available Options menu will be displayed.

2. Highlight Edit Print Job Configuration and press Enter. The Edit Print Job Configurations list is displayed.

3. Highlight the print job configuration you want to delete and press Delete.

4. A confirmation box now appears asking you to confirm your deletion choice. Highlight Yes and press Enter.

Renaming a Print Job Configuration

To rename a print job configuration, follow these steps:

1. At the DOS prompt, type PRINTCON Enter. The Available Options menu will be displayed.

2. Highlight Edit Print Job Configurations and press Enter. The Edit Print Job Configurations list will be displayed.

3. Highlight the print job configuration to be renamed and press the Modify key (Press F1 to verify the Modify key for your computer). The Change Name to box is displayed.

4. Use the Backspace key to delete the old name. Type in the new name and press Enter.

Editing a Print Job Configuration

To edit a print job configuration follow these steps:

1. At the DOS prompt, type PRINTCON Enter. The Available Options menu is displayed.

2. Highlight Edit Print Job Configurations and press Enter. The Edit Print Job Configurations list is displayed.

3. Highlight the print job configuration you want to edit and press Enter. The Edit Print Job Configuration screen is displayed (see Fig. 7-5). Table 7-2 defines all of the parameters in this screen.

4. Edit this screen by using the arrow keys to highlight the field you wish to change and pressing Enter. Type in the new value or select a value from the menu provided for that field. Press Enter to save the change.

5. When you have completed the print job configuration, press Escape.

6. To save your changes, highlight Yes and press Enter.

Selecting the Default Print Job Configuration

Only supervisors or supervisor equivalents can select the default print job configuration. The default print job configuration is the default for all jobs printed unless a flag is specified to override the default settings (see "Printing from the Command Line" at the end of this chapter). To select a default print job configuration, follow these steps:

1. At the DOS prompt, type PRINTCON Enter. The Available Options menu will be displayed.

2. Highlight Select Default Print Job Configuration and press Enter. The Select Default Print Job Configuration list will be displayed.

3. Highlight the print job configuration you are selecting as the default configuration and press Enter.

Copying Print Job Configurations

All print job configurations defined by a user are stored in one file called PRINTCON.DAT. This file is stored in the user's MAIL directory. Only a supervisor can copy the PRINTCON.DAT file from one user to another. (You must copy the whole file which contains all of the print job configurations created by the user. You cannot copy just one file.) When a PRINTCON.DAT file is copied from one user to another, it overwrites the target user's existing PRINTCON.DAT file. This erases all the print job configurations created by that user in his own file.

To copy a print job configuration follow these steps:

1. At the DOS prompt, type PRINTCON Enter. The Available Options menu is displayed (see Fig. 7-6).

2. Highlight Supervisor—Copy Print Job Configurations and press Enter.

3. In the Source User box, type the name of the source user (the user whose file you want to copy) and press Enter.

4. In the Target User box, type the name of the target user (the user you are copying the file to) and press Enter.

Fig. 7-6. Pconsole main menu

PCONSOLE

The Pconsole menu utility controls printing on your network. The supervisor must designate users and print queue operators in Pconsole. If you are a user, Pconsole allows you to change the print configuration of jobs you have sent to be printed, delete a job you have sent to print, view information about print queues, and see what jobs are waiting to be printed in a queue. A print queue operator can do all these plus he can edit any user's print configuration, delete any job from a queue, modify a queue, place a job on hold, and rearrange the order of jobs in a queue. Both users and print queue operators can attach to additional file servers and print from them if they have a login name and password for the additional server.

Attaching to Another File Server

You can use the following procedure to attach to another file server.

1. At the DOS prompt, type PCONSOLE and press Enter. You now see the Pconsole Available Options menu.

2. Highlight Change Current File Server and press Enter. You have a list of the file servers you are currently attached to and the user name you gave to access the file server.

3. Press Insert to see the Other File Servers list.

4. Highlight the file server you want to attach to and press Enter. You are asked for your user name and password for that file server. After entering this information, your screen displays the list of file servers to which you are attached. The new server you have just selected is now on the list.

Logging Out of Another File Server

You can also use Pconsole logout of other file servers. Use the following procedure to do this.

1. Type PCONSOLE at the DOS prompt and press Enter. You see the Available Option menu.

2. Highlight Change Current File Server and press Enter. Now you see a list of the file servers you are currently attached to.

3. Highlight the file server you wish to log out of and press delete. Answer Yes in the confirmation box. You are now logged out of that file server.

4. To delete several file servers at once use your Mark key to highlight each serve you are deleting (press F1 twice to verify the Mark key on your computer) and press Delete. When the Logout From All Marked Servers screen appears, highlight Yes and press Enter.
    NOTE: You cannot log out of your current default server or your primary server.

Changing Your User Name on Currently Attached Servers

If you need to access information on another file server using a different username and password than the one you originally used to attach to the server, you do not need to log out and then back in to the server. You can make the change in the File Server/User Name list by doing the following:

1. Type PCONSOLE Enter at the DOS prompt.

2. Highlight Change Current File Server and press Enter. You are in the File Server/User Name screen.

3. Highlight the file server on which you are changing your user name and press the Modify key (press F1 twice to verify the Modify key on your computer). Now you see the New User Name screen.

4. Type in the new user name and press enter. If a password is required you will be asked for it. The new user name now appears in the File Server/User Name screen.

Print Queues in Pconsole

When you send a job to print, it is sent to the selected print queue to wait until the printer is available. Using the Pconsole menu utility, you can list the print queues to see what jobs are waiting, add a print job, modify the job configuration, delete print jobs, change the order of print jobs in a queue, and place a print job on hold in the queue.

Listing Print Queues and the Waiting Jobs

The following procedure describes the procedure to list queues and jobs waiting to be printed.

1. Type PCONSOLE Enter at the DOS prompt. You are in the Available Options menu.

2. Highlight Print Queue Information and press Enter. You will see a list of the print queues defined on the file server to which you are currently defaulted.

3. To see which jobs are still waiting to be printed in a specific queue, highlight the queue and press Enter. You are now in the Print Queue Information menu.

4. Highlight Current Print Job Entries and press Enter. Now you have a list of the jobs which are waiting to be printed in that queue.

Adding a Print Job to a Queue

If you wish to print a job using one of the Printcon configurations you have set up, you must do so through Pconsole. To send a job to be printed using Pconsole follow these steps:

1. Type PCONSOLE Enter at the DOS prompt. You will be in the Available Options menu.

2. Highlight Print Queue Information and press Enter. You have accessed the Print Queues menu.

3. Highlight the print queue you wish to use to send the job and press Enter. You are now in the Print Queue Information menu.

4. Highlight Current Print Job Entries and press Enter. You now see the contents of the queue.

5. Press Insert to add a job to the queue. You now have the Select Directory to Print From screen. It displays your current directory path. If the job you wish to print is in the directory that is being displayed, press Enter. If the job is in another directory and you know the complete directory path, backspace the incorrect information out of the Select Directory to Print From screen, type in the correct information, and press Enter. If you do not know the complete path, do the following from the Select Directory to Print From screen:

   • Backspace all of the information out of the Select Directory to Print From screen and press Insert. You now see a list of available file servers.
   • Highlight the file server you are to print from and press Enter. The file server you have selected will now be displayed in the Select Directory to Print From screen and you will see a list of volumes to choose from.
   • Highlight the volume you wish and press Enter. The file server and volume you have chosen will be displayed in the Select Directory to Print From screen, and you will have a list of NetWork Directories.
   • Highlight the directory that contains the job and press Enter. The directory has been added to the Select Directory to Print From screen. Continue in this manner, selecting lower level subdirectories, until the entire directory path is displayed in the Select Directory to Print From screen.

6. Now press Enter and the Available Files list will appear.

7. Highlight the file you want to print and press Enter. You will see the Print Job Configurations menu. If you have defined any jobs in Printcon they are listed here, otherwise you only see (Pconsole Defaults).

8. Highlight the job configuration you wish to use and press Enter. You are in the New Print Job to be Submitted menu. This menu provides a number of parameters. They allow you to: specify the configurations of the job you are to print, change its priority in the queue, specify the date and time you want the job to print, change forms, specify whether or not you want a banner with the job, how many copies of the job are to be printed, and whether you wish to put the job on hold. These parameters are explained in Table 7-3.

NOTE: The job entry date and time, print job number, file size, and client name cannot be changed.

Table 7-3. New Print Job to be Submitted Parameters

Parameter	Description
Description	You can enter a description of the file you wish to print or make notes about the file. If you do not enter anything, you will get the default which is the file name.
User Hold	You can put the job on hold and it will not be printed until the parameter is changed back. This can be done by a user for their own jobs in the queue or by a print queue operator for any job in the queue. To put a print job on hold type Y. To remove a job from hold type N.
Operator Hold	If a job is put on hold by a print queue operator (by typing Y), it must also be removed by a print queue operator (by typing N).
Service Sequence	The service sequence is the position of the print job in the queue. Only a queue operator can change the order of the job in the queue.
Number of copies	You can tell Novell how many copies of the job you want printed.
File contents	You have a choice of whether to print Text or Byte Stream. Choose Text when you want Novell to interpret the coding and formatting or when you have a job that was not created by application software (such as a job in ASCII) and Byte Stream when you are printing a job which was created by application software and you want the software to handle the formatting.

Table 7-3 Ends.

Parameter	Description
Tab size	If you chose Text for your File Contents parameter you can use the Tab Size to specify how many spaces you want for the tabs in your print job. The default is 8.
Suppress form feed	If you accept the default, which is No, the printer advances to the top of the next page after you print your job. If you change the default to Yes, the printer does not advance to the next page.
Defer printing	If you want the job to be printed in its turn in the queue, leave the default set to No. If you want to print the job at a later date or time, choose Yes. You can then enter a Target date and Target time for the job to be printed.
Target server	You can specify which print server will print the job. If it doesn't matter, leave the default set to No.
Form	You can choose which of the forms defined in Printdef that you want to use for the job. In order to see a list of forms highlight Form and press Enter.
Print banner	If you want a banner to print before the job, choose Yes. If not, leave the default at No.
Banner name	If you decide to print a banner you can enter any text you want in the Banner name box. It will be printed in the first print area of the banner. The default is your username.
Banner file	If you decide to print a banner, you can enter any text you want in the Banner file box. It will print in the second print area of the banner. The default is the print job filename.
Target date	Enter the date you want your job printed. This option is only available if you have changed Defer printing to Yes.
Target time	Enter the time you want your job printed. This option is only available if you have changed Defer printing to Yes.

9. Once you have made your changes to the New Print Job to be Submitted menu, press Esc and the Save Changes confirmation screen will appear.

10. Highlight Yes and press Enter to add the job to the queue.

Changing the Parameters of a Job in the Queue

If you are a user, you can only change the parameters of your own print jobs while it is still in the queue. The print queue operator, however, can change anyone's print job parameters. To change the parameters of a print job in the queue, do the following:

1. Type PCONSOLE Enter at the DOS prompt. You are in the Available Options menu.

2. Highlight Print Queue Information and press Enter. You now see a list of the print queues.

3. Highlight the print queue you wish to access and press Enter. You are looking at the Print Queue Information menu.

4. Highlight Current Print Job Entries and press Enter. You will see a list of jobs in the print queue.

5. Highlight the job you wish to modify and press Enter. Use your arrow keys and the Enter key to highlight and change parameters.

6. Press Esc twice to exit and display the Save Changes confirmation screen.

7. Highlight Yes and press Enter to save the changes.

Cancelling a Print Job

To cancel a print job, you must either have sent the job to the queue or you must be a print queue operator. To cancel a job, do the following:

1. Type PCONSOLE Enter at the DOS prompt. You are in the Available Options menu.

2. Highlight Print Queue Information and press Enter. You now have a list of the print queues.

3. Highlight the print queue you wish to access and press Enter. You see the Print Queue Information menu.

4. Highlight Current Print Job Entries and press Enter. All of the print jobs in the queue are displayed.

5. Highlight the job you wish to cancel and press Delete. The Delete Queue Entry screen will appear.

6. Highlight Yes and press Enter. The job will be cancelled.

Changing the Job Order in a Queue

You must be a print queue operator to change the order of print jobs in a queue. It is done through the Print Queue Entry Information menu. To make this change, do the following:

1. Type PCONSOLE Enter at the DOS prompt. You are in the Available Options menu.

2. Highlight Print Queue Information and press Enter. You now see a list of the print queues.

3. Highlight the queue you want to access and press Enter. You are in the Print Queue Information menu.

4. Highlight Current Print Job Entries and press Enter. You have a list of all the jobs in the queue.

5. Highlight the print job you want to move and press Enter. Now you see the Print Queue Entry Information menu.

6. Move your cursor to Service Sequence. Now type in a number to indicate the position in the queue the print is to have. Press Enter and then Esc.

Viewing and Changing the Print Queue Status

Any user can view the status of a print queue, but you must be a print queue operator to change the status of any of the parameters in the queue.

1. Type PCONSOLE Enter at the DOS prompt. You are in the Available Options menu.

2. Highlight Print Queue Information and press Enter. You see a list of the print queues.

3. Highlight the queue whose status you wish to view or change and press Enter. You are at the Print Queue Information menu.

4. Highlight Current Queue Status and press Enter. The Current Queue Status screen is displayed. This screen displays the number of entries in the queue, the number of servers attached to the queue, and the operator flag information. If you are a print queue operator, you can change the flags (see Table 7-4) by using your cursor arrow keys to move to the flag you wish to change, typing Y for yes or N for no, and then pressing Enter. When you have made all of your changes, press Esc to exit and save.

Table 7-4. Operator Flag Descriptions

Operator Flags	Description
Users Can Place Entries in Queue	If the print queue operator sets this flag to no, users cannot send any jobs to the queue until the flag has been reset to yes.
Server Can Service Entries in Queue	If this flag is set to no, the print servers are not allowed to process print jobs in the queue until the flag has been reset to yes.
New Servers Can Attach to Queue	If this flag is set to no, new servers are not allowed to attach to the print queue until the flag has been reset to yes.

Viewing the Print Queue Servers

1. Type PCONSOLE Enter at the DOS prompt. You are in the Available Options menu.

2. Highlight Print Queue Information and press Enter. You now see a list of print queues.

3. Highlight the queue you want to access and press Enter. The Print Queue Information menu appears.

4. Highlight Queue Servers and press Enter. The Print Queue Servers screen is displayed.

Remember: The queue must be attached to the print server in order for the server to service the queue.

Listing the Queue Users

1. Type PCONSOLE Enter at the DOS prompt. You are in the Available Options menu.

2. Highlight Print Queue Information and press Enter. You see a list of print queues.

3. Highlight the print queue you wish to access and press Enter. You now see the Print Queue Information menu.

4. Highlight Queue Users and press Enter. The Queue Users screen lists the groups and users who can send jobs to the queue.

Listing the Print Servers

1. Type PCONSOLE Enter at the DOS prompt. You are in the Available Options menu.

2. Highlight Print Server Information and press Enter. You now see a list of your print servers. This option only applies to file servers.

Viewing the Print Server's Full Name

1. Type PCONSOLE Enter at the DOS prompt. You are in the Available Options menu.

2. Highlight Print Server Information and press Enter. You now have a list of print servers.

3. Highlight the server you wish to view and press Enter. You see the Print Server Information screen.

4. Highlight Full Name and press Enter. The print server's full name is displayed.

Viewing the Print Server's ID

1. Type PCONSOLE Enter at the DOS prompt. You are in the Available Options menu.

2. Highlight Print Server Information and press Enter. You will see the Print Server Names list.

3. Highlight the server whose ID you want to view and press Enter. You now have the Print Server Information screen.

4. Highlight Print Server ID and press Enter. The server's ID number will be displayed.

Creating a Print Queue

1. Type PCONSOLE Enter at the DOS prompt. You are in the Available Topics menu.

2. Highlight Print Queue Information and press Enter. You are now in the Print Queues screen.

3. Press Insert to see the New Print Queue Name screen.

4. Type in the name of the queue you want to create and press Enter. The new print queue now appears in the Print Queues screen.

Deleting a Print Queue

1. Type PCONSOLE Enter at the DOS prompt. You are in the Available Topics menu.

2. Highlight Print Queue Information and press Enter. You are in the Print Queues screen.

3. Highlight the queue you wish to delete and press Delete. Confirm the deletion and press Enter.

PRINTING FROM THE COMMAND LINE

When using application software that recognizes NetWare printers, you can direct your print jobs through the software. However, not all applications software recognize network printers. Many of them only recognize local printers. In these situations, it is necessary to redirect the local printer to the network printer through the Novell command line utilities. In addition, you might want to specify other options not included with the software.

Capture

The Capture command is used to redirect print from a local printer to a network printer. For example, to redirect a job to the network printer 0, type this at the command line:

CAPTURE L1 P0

You can use the flags shown in Table 7-5 with the Capture command.

Table 7-5. Capture Flag Options

Flag	Description
Show(SH)	This flag displays the file server, the queue, and the printer to which the local printer has been redirected. Do not use this flag with any other Capture flags.
Autoendcap(A)	You use this flag to send data to a network printer or file when you enter or exit an application. The Autoendcap command leaves the local printer redirected to the network printer until you reverse it with Endcap. Autoendcap is a default setting.
Noautoendcap(NA)	This flag prevents data from being sent to a network printer or file when you enter or exit an application.
Timeout(TI)=n	This flag enables Timeout. The n represents the number (between 1 through 1,000) of seconds that pass between the time you execute the print command in the application software and the moment the job is queued for printing. The default for Timeout is TI=0, which means Timeout is disabled unless you include it in your Capture command. The Capture command, used with Timeout, looks like this: CAPTURE L1 P0 TI=5
Local(L)=n	You use this flag to indicate which LPT (or local) port you want to Capture. Replace n with 1, 2, or 3. The default is LPT1. This flag can be entered in the following ways: CAPTURE L=1 P=0 TI=5 CAPTURE L1 P0 TI=5
Server(S)=server	This flag tells the Capture command which file server to send the data to for printing. The default is your default server.
Job(J)=job	Use this flag to indicate a specific print job configuration (refer to the "Printcon" section earlier in this chapter for a complete explanation of print job configurations). Users, print queue operators, and supervisors all can use Printcon to define print jobs.

Table 7-5 Continued.

Flag	Description
Printer(P)=n	This flag specifies which network printer you want to redirect the local printer. The default is printer 0.
Queue(Q)=queue	This flag indicates which print queue to send the data. The Capture command used with the Queue flag looks like this:

```
CAPTURE L1 P0 TI=5 Q=PRINTQ_0
```

Flag	Description
Form(F)=form or n	This flag specifies the form (type and size of paper) your job is to be printed on. Replace form with the name of the form or n with the number of the form you wish to use. Forms are defined in Printdef, covered earlier in this chapter.
Copies=n	This flag specifies the number of copies you need of the current print job. The n is a number between 1 and 256.
Tabs(T)=n	Use this flag only if your application software does not have a print formatter. Replace the n with the number of spaces you want for each tab.
Notabs(NT)	Use this flag only if your application software does not have a print formatter. The flag ensures that all tabs in your job arrive at the printer unchanged.
Name(NAM)=name	If you are printing a banner, with your print job, this flag specifies the username to appear on the banner. The default is the username you logged in with.
Banner(B)=banner	This flag specifies the banner word that is to appear at the bottom of your banner. Replace banner with any word or phrase you wish up to 12 characters long. You cannot use spaces. If you want to separate words, replace spaces with an underline.
Nobanner(NB)	This flag specifies that no banner is to be printed.
Formfeed(FF)	This flag enables a form feed after your job has printed. The Formfeed flag causes Novell to force a blank page at the end of every print job.

Table 7-5 Ends.

Flag	Description
Noformfeed(NFF)	This flag disables the automatic form feed at the end of the print job.
Create(CR)=filespec	This flag allows you to send the print job to a file, instead of a printer. Replace filespec with the path and name of the file to which you are directing the print job.
Keep(K)	This flag causes the server to keep the data it received from your workstation. In the event your workstation freezes or loses power, fifteen minutes after freezing or a power loss, the file server sends the data it received to a printer.

The Capture command is typed at the DOS prompt before you enter the software application. It can be included in your Novell menu (see Chapter 6).

Endcap

This command ends the Capture of a local printer. Table 7-6 shows the flags you can use with Endcap.

Endcap is used only after a Capture command has been given, and it should be placed on a separate line.

Table 7-6. Endcap Flag Options

Flag	Description
Local(L)=n	This flag ends the Capture of a specific local port. Replace n with 1, 2 or 3. Your command will look like this: ENDCAP L=1
All	This flag ends the capture of all LPT ports.
Cancel	This flag ends the capture of the current print job and discards the data from the current job without printing it.

Table 7-6 Ends.

Flag	Description
Cancellocal=n	This flag ends the capture of a specified LPT port and discards all data in that port without printing it. Replace n with 1, 2 or 3.
Cancel all	This flag ends the capture of all LPT ports and discards all the data without printing it.

Nprint

Nprint sends files to a network printer. Filespec represents the path and name of the file you wish to print. The flags available for this command are shown in Table 7-7.

NOTE: No Nprint command can exceed 128 characters.

Table 7-7. Nprint Flag Options

Flag	Description
Server(S)=server	This flag indicates the file server from which the file is to be printed. Replace the variable server with the name of a file server.
Job(J)=job	This flag specifies the name of the print job configuration you are using (see Printcon earlier in this chapter).
Printer(P)=n	This flag specifies the network printer to which the file is to be sent. The variable, n, represents the number of the printer. The default printer is 0.
Queue(Q)=queue	This flag specifies the print queue to which the file is to be sent. Replace the variable, queue, with the name of the print queue you are using (example: QUEUE =PRINTQ_0).
Form(F)=form or n	This flag indicates a specific form (type of paper) you want to use to print your file. Replace the variable, form, with the name of the form or, if you are using form numbers, n, with the number of the form you wish to use.

Table 7-7 Ends.

Flag	Description
Copies=n	This flag specifies how many copies of the file you wish to print. The variable, n, can be any number between 1 and 256.
Tabs(T)=n	Use this flag only if your application software is unable to format a job for printing. The variable, n, represents the number of spaces you want for each tab.
Notabs(NT)	Use this flag only if your application software is incapable of print formatting. It ensures that the tabs in your print job will print unchanged.
Name(NAM)=name	This flag indicates the username that will appear on the top half of your banner. The default is the username with which you logged in.
Banner(B)=banner	This flag specifies the banner word you want to appear on the bottom half of your banner. Replace the variable, banner, with any word that is no longer than 12 characters. You cannot use spaces in the banner word. The default banner is the name of the file you are printing.
Nobanner(NB)	This flag specifies that no banner will be printed with the print file.
Formfeed(FF)	This flag enables form feed after your file has been printed. The default is form feed enabled.
Noformfeed(NFF)	This flag disables form feed.
Delete	This flag automatically erases a file after it has been printed.

NOTE: The Nprint command cannot exceed 128 characters.

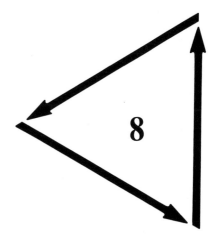

8

Monitoring and Communicating through Terminals

Even though ABC Company's network is set up and operating, there is still a lot of work for the network supervisor. He or she must continuously monitor the performance of the network. By this we mean the supervisor must manage the network resources: he must ensure the hard drive is not running out of space, verify the network is being used to maximum advantage, and make changes necessary to maximize performance. He needs to know the peak periods, when the network is being used most heavily, and the slow periods.

This information makes it possible to schedule the massive data sorting and other large jobs that tax network resources to a time when the network is not as heavily used. This balances the use of the network resources. This ensures that all jobs are done in the fastest and most efficient manner. Novell has provided several utilities to help a supervisor monitor the use of a network. One of the most helpful is Fconsole.

FCONSOLE?

Fconsole is the menu utility you use to obtain a complete picture of the network's performance. By using Fconsole, you are able to determine when the network is used most heavily, how many users are attached to the network, how much memory is being used at any given time, and how many indexed files can be used at one time. Fconsole also allows you to change file servers, broadcast messages, purge files, and, if necessary, bring down a file server and clear a user's connection to the server.

To access Fconsole, type FCONSOLE at the DOS prompt. You now see the menu shown in Fig. 8-1.

Let us review the options in the Available Topics menu.

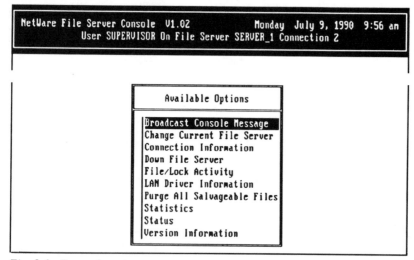

Fig. 8-1. Fconsole main menu

Broadcast Console Message

The first utility on the Available Topics menu is Broadcast Console Message. This option is used by console operators, supervisors or supervisor equivalents to send messages to all stations currently logged into the network. There is a limit of 55 characters per message. To send a message, highlight Broadcast Console Message and press Enter. At the Message: prompt type in the message you wish to send (remember you are limited to a maximum of 55 characters) and press Enter.

If you wish to send a message to an individual user, you may do so through the Session menu utility. At the DOS prompt, type SESSION.

1. Highlight User List in the Available Topics menu and press Enter.

2. Highlight the user to wish to sent to in the Current Users list and press Enter.

3. Highlight Send Message in the Available Topics menu and press Enter. You see a prompt Message: From SUPERVISOR:, if you are a supervisor, or your user name in place of SUPERVISOR.

4. Type in the message you wish to send and press Enter.

Change Current File Server

This option permits you to select another file server as the network default server or to log in to or out of other file servers. To access this option, highlight Change Current File Server in the Available Topics menu and press Enter. You now see a list of the file server you are currently logged into and the user name you used.

To choose another server as the default server, highlight the server you want to change to and press Enter. You have now changed to another server. This new server is now the default server.

To log on to another file server:

1. From the Change Current File Server menu, press Enter. A list of available file servers now appears on the screen.

2. Highlight the server you want to log on to and press Enter. You will see a User Name: prompt. Type your user name and press Enter. If you have specified a password with your user name, you see a Password: prompt. Type in your password, and press Enter.

3. The name of the new file server will now appear in the file server list. To change to this server, highlight it and press Enter.

To log out of a filer server:

1. Highlight the file server you wish to log out of and press delete.

2. You now have a confirmation screen. Highlight Yes and press Enter. The specified server is no longer listed in the file server list.

To change to a different user name on a file server:

1. Press the Modify Key (press F1 twice to verify the Modify Key on your computer). A screen with the prompt New User Name: appears.

2. Type in the user name you want to change to and press Enter. If the new user name requires a password, you get the following prompt: Password:.

3. Type in your password and press Enter.

If changing to a different user on the file server would cause files or drives you are currently using under the old user name to be lost when the old user logs out, you get an error message saying Default User Cannot Be Changed. If this occurs, press Escape. You are returned to the file server list. You must then either log out of the files or drives you are currently using or keep the old user name.

Connection Information

This option gives you a list of all connections to the current file server. If you are a console operator, a supervisor, or a supervisor equivalent, this option gives you detailed information about the status of each connection. If you are a user, you are limited to viewing the name and connection number of other users who are logged in.

To view current user connections highlight Connection Information and press Enter. Figure 8-2 shows the Current Connections screen.

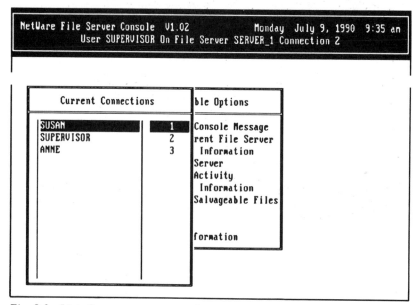

```
NetWare File Server Console  V1.02              Monday  July 9, 1990  9:35 am
                User SUPERVISOR On File Server SERVER_1 Connection 2


        Current Connections          ble Options

      SUSAN                   1     Console Message
      SUPERVISOR              2     rent File Server
      ANNE                    3      Information
                                    Server
                                    Activity
                                     Information
                                    Salvageable Files

                                    formation
```

Fig. 8-2. List of current user connections

You must have either console operator or supervisor privileges to view any more information about a connection to the server. If you are a supervisor, highlight the user name to get information about and press Enter. The Connection Information menu (Fig. 8-3) is now on your screen.

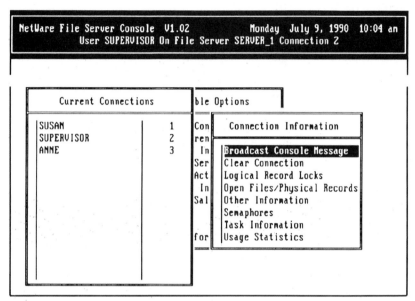

Fig. 8-3. Connection information menu for selected user

Broadcast Console Message   If you wish to broadcast a message to several connections at the same time:

1. Use your Mark Key (press F1 twice to verify the Mark key on your computer) to select the connections.

2. Highlight Broadcast Console Message and press Enter.

3. When the Message: prompt appears, type your message and press Enter.

Clear Connection   This allows a supervisor or supervisor equivalent to clear a connection to the file server. If you clear a user's connection to the file server, you have effectively logged him out of the server. If the user was in a program, that program aborts. This option is to be used with care. To clear a connection:

1. Highlight the Clear Connection option and press Enter.

2. When the confirmation box appears on the screen highlight Yes and press Enter.

Logical Record Locks   The Logical Record Locks option displays all logical record locks the selected connection has logged with the server. It also displays what task is using the lock and the lock type.

This option is used by programs to control data file access to only one user at a time. When the first user accesses a data file, Novell and the application program lock the file. When another user attempts to access the same data, the program discovers that it has been locked by another station. The second user must wait for the first to finish using the data and unlock it. Then the next user can access the data. If a program does not have the locking convention written into it, the logical lock is not enforced. Multiple users can access and use the same data simultaneously.

To view the Logical Records Lock option, highlight it and press Enter. You are in the Logical Records Lock menu. This menu allows you to see the lock and log status of a logical record. There are several different status messages that this menu displays. They are:

Logged. The station has included the record in a list of records it wants to lock as a set. This avoids an impasse with other stations that might want to lock the same records.

Locked Shareable. This message means that other stations may also lock the record shareable, but no other station can lock the record exclusively. This mode is generally used when reading data another station shouldn't change.

Locked Exclusively. This message means that no other station can lock the record. This mode is generally used when a station is changing data and no other station should be reading or updating the data.

Being held by the Transaction Track System. If data is being updated in a file that is transaction tracked, the file server maintains exclusive locks until the entire transaction is complete. This allows the transaction to be backed out in case the workstation, the network, or the file server should fail during the transaction.

Open Files/Physical Records   This option displays all files currently being used by the selected connection. You can see a file status along with any physical record locks the connection has in the file.

To use this option highlight Open Files/Physical Records and press Enter. Figure 8-4 shows the Files In Use screen.

If you wish to see the file status or physical record locks of a particular file, highlight that file and press Enter. A menu appears with two options.

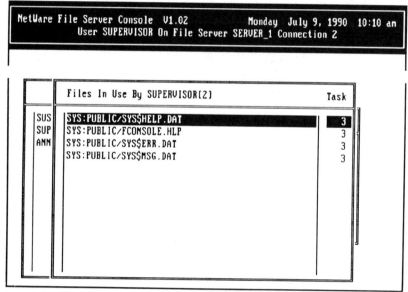

Fig. 8-4. List of files in use by supervisor

To view the status of a file highlight File Status and press Enter. You now get a window giving you the status of that file. The status messages this option contains are:

Open. The workstation has the file open.

Open in Share Mode. The workstation has the file open, and it is flagged shareable.

Not Open. The workstation does not have the file open.

Open for Read Only. The workstation has requested read access to the file.

Open for Write Only. The workstation has requested write access to the file.

Open for Read and Write. The workstation has requested both read and write access to the file.

Allow Reads and Writes from Other Stations. The workstation is allowing other stations to read and write to the file.

Deny Reads, but Allow Writes from Other Stations. The workstation is not allowing other stations to read from the file, but is allowing them to write to it.

Allow Reads, but Deny Writes from Other Stations. The workstation is allowing other stations to read from the file, but writing is not allowed.

Deny Reads and Writes from Other Stations. The workstation is not allowing other stations to read or write to the file.

Locked by Shared File Set Transaction. The file is locked as part of a shared file set transaction.

Locked by File Lock. The file is locked.

File is Detached (No I/O is Permitted until File is Locked). The workstation must relock the file before access is allowed to it.

File is Logged. The workstation has logged the file.

To access the second option, highlight Physical Record Locks and press Enter. A window appears listing all the files used by that connection and the physical locks in the file.

Other Information   This option tells you what user is logged into a connection as well as when and where he logged in.

Semaphores   Semaphores are used to limit how many tasks a resource can use at one time. They also limit the number of workstations that can run the same program simultaneously. When you choose this option, a window appears showing the semaphore name, the task using it, the number of connections using it, and the value. The value specifies the number of workstations allowed to use the resource at the same time.

Task Information   The Task Information menu tells you which tasks are active at the connection's workstation. It will also tell you if the station is waiting for a lock or a semaphore.

Usage Statistics   Usage Statistics tell you how long a user has been logged on to the server, the number of requests the user has sent to the file server, the number of bytes the connection has read, and the number of bytes the connection has written since logging on.

Down File Server

To down a filer server, you must be a supervisor or supervisor equivalent. When you down a file server, all users are excluded from the server until you bring the server back up. It is advisable, therefore, to broadcast a message to all connections requesting them to log out before you down the server. To down the server, highlight Down File Server and press Enter.

File/Lock Activity

You must be a console operator, a supervisor or a supervisor equivalent to use this option. It allows you to view all the connections currently using a file. It also gives you the file's status information and the use of locks and semaphores. You access this option by highlighting File/Lock Activity and pressing Enter. A menu now appears showing three options: File/Physical Records Information, Logical Lock Information, and Semaphore Information.

To view information about a file:

1. Highlight File/Physical Records Information and press Enter.

2. At the prompt Directory Path (excluding the file name) type the directory path that contains the file you need information on and press Enter.

3. When the File Name: prompt appears, type in the name of the file and press Enter.

4. You now have a menu with two options: File Status, and Physical Records Lock.

5. Highlight File Status and press Enter to see the status of a file. A window opens telling you the number of connections using the file, how many connections have the file open for reading and writing, how many connections have opened the file and denied reading or writing privileges to other stations, and the lock status of the file.

6. Highlight Physical Records Lock and press Enter to view any physical locks that any connection has on the file. This option shows the file's directory path and the number and type of locks on the file.

The Logical Lock Information option permits you to view all the connections using a logical record lock and the status of the lock. It tells you the numbers of connections having the logical record lock, and if it is locked shareable, locked exclusive, or not locked.

The Semaphore Information option will tell you how many connections have the semaphore in use, which connections they are, the number of the task that is using the semaphore, and the value of the semaphore.

LAN Driver Information

This option shows the configuration for the LAN drivers selected for the file server. It tells you the network address, the address of the interface board for the network, the type of interface board being used by the network, and the configuration of the interface board. This information is useful for avoiding network address conflicts when installing new workstations or bridges.

Purge All Salvageable Files

You must be a console operator, a supervisor, or a supervisor equivalent to use this option. A salvageable file is one deleted by a user. The system temporarily keeps the file in case it was deleted by accident. These files occupy space and directory entries on your hard drive. If you are low on space or directory entries, use this option to delete all of the salvageable files being held by the system.

Statistics

This option gives you information about how the file server is performing. To access this option, highlight Statistics and press Enter. The File Server Statistics menu (Fig. 8-5) is now on your screen.

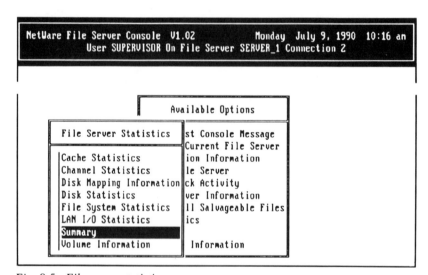

Fig. 8-5. File server statistics menu

Cache Statistics This option allows you to view information about the network's disk caching performance. When Novell was installed, each cache buffer was automatically partitioned into blocks of 4,096 bytes each. The number of cache buffers on your network is determined by the amount of memory your file server has. Caching increases the performance of your network by reading each request to the network in a cache buffer (holding it in memory). The more information that can be held in memory, the more efficiently the network operates because the system does not have to go to the disk to access the information. The Cache Statistics window will tell you the following:

Number of Cache Buffers. This is the number of cache buffers your file server has.

Cache Buffer Size. This is the size of your cache buffers. It is automatically set by Novell at installation to 4,096 bytes.

Dirty Cache Buffers. This is the number of cache buffers containing information not yet written to disk.

Cache Read Requests. This indicates the number of times the cache buffer software has been asked to read from the disk.

Cache Write Requests. This shows the number of times the cache buffer software has been asked to write to the disk.

Cache Hits. This is the number of times a request was accessed from an existing cache block.

Cache Misses. This gives the number of times a request could not be accessed from an existing cache block, which necessitated allocating another cache block.

Physical Read Requests. This shows the number of times the cache buffer software was asked to read information from the disk to a cache buffer.

Physical Write Requests. The number of times the cache buffer software was asked to write information from a cache buffer to the disk.

Cache Get Requests. This is the total of the Cache Read Requests and the Cache Write Requests. It represents the total number of times the cache buffer software retrieved information from or wrote information to the disk.

Full Write Requests. This shows the number of times the cache buffer software wrote information to the disk that filled one or more sectors exactly (a sector is 512 bytes).

Partial Write Requests. This is the number of times the cache buffer software wrote information to the disk that did not exactly fill a sector.

Background Dirty Writes. This gives the number of times a full cache block has been written to the disk.

Background Aged Writes. This shows the number of times a partially filled cache block has been written to disk.

Total Cache Writes. This is the total number of entire cache blocks written to disk.

Cache Allocations. This shows the number of times a cache block has been allocated for use.

Thrashing Count. This gives the number of times a cache block was not available because all the cache blocks were in use by the system.

LRU Block Was Dirty. This expresses the number of times the requested data was not in memory and the cache block, which the system allocated, contained data that had to be written to the disk to allow the cache block to be allocated.

Read Beyond Write. This represents the number of times a read request asked for data not yet read into an allocated cache block, requiring that the cache buffer software had to go to the disk to get the data.

Fragmented Writes. This is the number of times a dirty cache buffer had to be written to the disk with more than one write request.

Hit on Unavailable Block. This indicates the number of times the requested data was in a cache buffer but could not be used because the data was in use.

Cache Blocks Scrapped. This gives the number of times a cache buffer that the system was going to allocate was scrapped.

Channel Statistics   Channel Statistics give you the addresses being used by the disk channel. This information is helpful when you are installing additional disk drives to avoid conflicts in setting addresses.

Disk Mapping Information   This option gives you information about the file server's disk drive mappings. If you chose the Disk Mapping Information option, you can view the level of system fault tolerance your Novell software supports. If you are using Advanced NetWare, you have a 1; if you are using SFT NetWare (which supports disk mirroring and duplexing), you have a 2. You can also view the number of access requests from the disk in Pending I/O Commands. You can determine the number of logical disks, the number of physical disks attached to the file server, the status of all disk channels, what physical disks are mapped to what logical disks for mirroring purposes, and the status of any drive that is not normal.

Disk Statistics   This option allows you to view information about each hard drive that is attached to the file server. The following information is shown:

Disk Type. This identifies the type of disk and whether or not the disk is removable.

Disk Channel. This is the number of the disk channel to which the disk is attached.

Controller Number. This gives the controller number on the disk channel that is being used to access the drive.

Drive Number. This shows the drive number on the controller that is being used to access the drive.

Controller Type. This identifies the type of controller for the disk.

Drive Size. This is the size of the disk drive in bytes. This does not include any bytes that might have been chosen for Hot Fix redirection (explained later in this chapter).

Drive Cylinders. This shows the number of cylinders on the drive.

Drive Heads. This gives the number of heads on the drive.

Sectors per Track. This gives the number of 512 byte sectors that are on each disk track.

I/O Error Count. This shows the number of errors that have occurred while accessing the drive.

Hot Fix   The Hot Fix function of NetWare works with the read-after-write verification. This means that, after data has been written to a disk, Hot Fix verifies the data on the disk matches the data in memory. If they do not match, Hot Fix sends the original block of data from memory to another area on the disk and stores it correctly. The operating system records the address of the defective block. Data is not stored there again.

The following Hot Fix status messages are available in Disk Statistics:

Hot Fix Table. This shows the start of the disk's Hot Fix table.

Hot Fix Enabled. If this feature is bold on your screen, Hot Fix is enabled.

Hot Fix Table Size. This gives the number of blocks set aside for Hot Fix use.

Hot Fix Remaining. This shows the number of blocks still remaining for Hot Fix use.

File System Statistics   Selecting File System Statistics tracks memory use in your system. Figure 8-6 shows the File System Statistics screen. The following information is on your screen:

Configured Max Open Files. This is the maximum number of files the file server can open simultaneously. This number can be changed by rerunning Netgen.

Peak Files Open. This is the largest number of files that the file server has opened simultaneously since it was last brought up. If this figure is close to the Configured Max Open Files figure, you should rerun Netgen to increase the number of Configured Max Open Files. (See the Novell NetWare manuals on how to do this.)

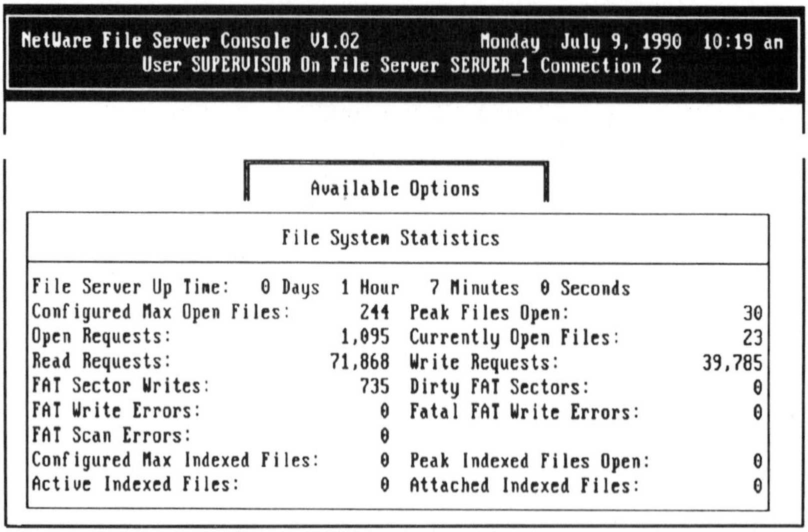

```
NetWare File Server Console  V1.02           Monday  July 9, 1990  10:19 am
                 User SUPERVISOR On File Server SERVER_1 Connection 2
```

```
┌────────────────────────────────────────┐
│            Available Options            │
│ ┌──────────────────────────────────────┤
│ │          File System Statistics       │
│ ├──────────────────────────────────────┤
│ │ File Server Up Time:   0 Days  1 Hour   7 Minutes  0 Seconds │
│ │ Configured Max Open Files:     244  Peak Files Open:         30 │
│ │ Open Requests:               1,095  Currently Open Files:    23 │
│ │ Read Requests:              71,868  Write Requests:      39,785 │
│ │ FAT Sector Writes:             735  Dirty FAT Sectors:       0 │
│ │ FAT Write Errors:                0  Fatal FAT Write Errors:  0 │
│ │ FAT Scan Errors:                 0                              │
│ │ Configured Max Indexed Files:    0  Peak Indexed Files Open:  0 │
│ │ Active Indexed Files:            0  Attached Indexed Files:   0 │
│ └──────────────────────────────────────┘
```

Fig. 8-6. File system statistics screen

Currently Open Files. This shows how many files are currently open on the file server. It reflects files opened both by users and the system itself.

Open Requests. This gives the number of requests to open a file the server has received since it was last brought up.

Read Requests. This is the number of requests to read from a file the server has received since it was last brought up.

Write Requests. This gives the number of requests to write to a file the server has received since it was last brought up.

FAT Sector Writes. This shows the number of times the server has written a sector containing File Allocation Table (FAT) information to the disk.

Dirty FAT Sectors. This is the number of sectors containing FAT information that have changed since they were last written to the disk.

FAT Write Errors. This indicates the number of times an attempt to write a changed FAT to the disk failed. Two copies of the FAT are kept on the disk to ensure this information is not lost.

Fatal FAT Writes Errors. This is the number of times a disk write error occurred in both the original and the duplicate of a FAT sector. The FAT tells the system where the files are located; loss of this information is considered a fatal error. FAT information is booted into memory when the system is brought up and stays resident until the system is brought down. If you see this message, back up all files immediately.

FAT Scan Errors. This shows the number of times an inconsistent state was detected in the server.

Configured Max Indexed Files. This gives the maximum number of FAT indexed files that can be opened simultaneously. FAT indexing can double or triple the speed to access a database file of more than one megabyte.

Peak Indexed Files Open. This is the maximum number of indexed files that have been opened at one time since the file server has been brought up.

Active Indexed Files. This is the number of currently active (opened) indexed files.

Attached Indexed Files. This shows the number of indexed files ready to be used but not currently open.

LAN I/O Statistics This option allows you to view statistics on the number of packets received and routed by the file server. This indicates how busy the network is. The information on this screen is explained below:

Total Packets Received. This gives the total number of packets received by the server since it was brought up.

Packets Routed. This is the number of packets the server has routed to another server since it was brought up.

NETBIOS Broadcasts. This shows how often NETBIOS packets have been rebroadcast by the server.

Packets With Invalid Slots. This is the number of packets received by the server from a connection not supported by the filer server.

Invalid Connections. This gives the number of packets, with an invalid connection number, received by the server. Usually, this only happens when the server is brought down before all stations have logged out.

Invalid Sequence Number. This is the number of times the server received a service request when the request sequence number has not been higher than the previous request.

Invalid Request Types. This indicates the number of requests with an unknown request type the server has received.

Detach with Invalid Slot. This shows the number of times the server has received a request to detach an invalid connection.

Forged Detach Requests. This tells the number of times the server has ignored a detach request from a station whose connection number does not match the connection number of the station at that address.

New Request During Processing. This is the number of new requests received by the server while a previous request is being processed.

New Attach During Processing. This gives the number of requests the server receives to attach a station for which the server is currently processing a request.

Ignored Duplicate Attach. This shows how often the server has received a duplicate attach request.

Reply Cancelled by New Attach. This is the number of times the server has cancelled a reply to a request because it received a new request to attach.

Detach During Processing Ignored. This indicates how often a request has been made to detach a station while a previous request is being processed. If this happens, the server ignores the request to detach and finishes processing the previous request.

Re-executed Request. This shows how often the server has re-executed a request.

Duplicate Replies Sent. This is the number of times the server has been asked to re-execute a request it did not have to do because the reply was still in memory.

Positive Acknowledges Sent. This shows how often the server has sent a message to a station acknowledging a previous request when that station sends a second request for the same service.

File Service Used Route. This is the number of times the server had to place a request in a routing buffer, because there were no service processes available when the request was received.

Packets Discarded Because They Crossed More Than 16 Bridges. This shows how many packets were thrown away because they had crossed more than 16 bridges and the packet was either lost or travelling in a circle.

Packets Discarded Because Destination Network Is Unknown. This is how many packets were thrown away, because they were sent to a network that cannot be found by the sending network.

Incoming Packets Lost Because of No Available Buffers. This gives the number of packets that could not be received because the network had no buffers available to receive them.

Outgoing Packets Lost Because of No Available Buffers. This is how many packets were lost by the network when it tried to send them because there were no routing buffers available.

Summary   The Summary is another very useful tool. With it you can determine if your network is working at optimum efficiency. You can get the following information:

File Server Up Time. This shows how long the server has been up for the current boot.

Number of File Service Processes. This tells how many requests can be processed simultaneously by the server.

Current Server Utilization. This is the percentage of time the CPU is being used by the file server.

Disk Requests Serviced from Cache. This gives the percentage of requests that are serviced by the cache buffers. The higher the percentage, the more efficiently your network will operate.

Packets Routed. This tells how many packets the server has routed in the last second.

Total Packets Received. This is the total number of requests for file services and routing received since the server was brought up.

File Service Packets. This gives the number of requests for file services the server has received since it was last brought up.

Total Number Buffers. This shows the total number of cache buffers in the server. The number of cache buffers can be changed by adding or deleting memory from the server. Generally, the more cache buffers you have in your network, the more efficiently your network operates.

Dirty Cache Buffers. This shows how many cache buffers containing information have not yet been written to disk, because they have not been filled.

Total Server Memory. This tells you how much memory is in your file server.

Unused Server Memory. This is the amount of memory in the file server that cannot be used by the network, because it is fragmented into small pieces.

Routing Buffers: Maximum. This is the total number of routing buffers in the file server. This number is determined during the Novell installation process.

Routing Buffers: Peak Used. This indicates the largest number of routing buffers used simultaneously since the server was last brought up.

Routing Buffers: Currently in Use. This shows how many routing buffers are currently being used by the server.

Open Files: Maximum. This is how many files can be opened simultaneously on the network.

Open Files: Peak Used. This shows the largest number of files that have been open at the same time since the server was last brought up.

Open Files: Currently in Use. This tells how many files are currently being used by the server.

Indexed Files: Maximum. This gives the greatest number of indexed files that can be opened and used simultaneously. Indexing a large database file loads its location into memory. This increases access time to the file dramatically.

Indexed Files: Peak Used. This shows the largest number of index files that have been in use since the server was last brought up.

Indexed Files: Currently in Use. This tells how many index files are now in use.

Transactions: Maximum. If your version of Novell supports transactional tracking, this option shows you the greatest number of transactions the system can track at one time.

Transactions: Peak Used. This is the greatest number of simultaneous transactions the system has tracked since the server was last brought up.

Transactions: Currently in Use. This is the number of transactions currently in use on the file server.

Bindery Objects: Maximum. This gives the maximum number of objects that can be created in the bindery. The bindery contains such objects as users, groups, print queues, and file servers. The number of bindery objects available on your network is determined during Novell installation. If, during installation, no limit was set you see "N/A" on the screen.

Bindery Objects: Peak Used. This shows the greatest number of bindery objects in use at once since the server was last brought up.

Bindery Objects: Currently in Use. This tells how many objects are currently existing in the bindery.

Connections: Maximum. This is the maximum number of workstations that can connect to the server at the same time. This number is determined by the version of Novell your network is running. It cannot be changed.

Connections: Peak Used. This is the greatest number of stations connected to the server simultaneously since it was last brought up.

Connections: Currently in Use. This tells how many stations are currently connected to the server.

Dynamic Memory 1: Maximum. This shows how much memory available in the first dynamic memory pool (there are three). The first dynamic memory pool is used for mapping directories and as a temporary buffer when a service request is being processed.

Dynamic Memory 1: Peak Used. This is the largest amount of memory from the first pool used simultaneously since the server was last brought up.

Dynamic Memory 1: Currently in Use. This says how much memory in the first pool is currently in use.

Dynamic Memory 2: Maximum. This is the total amount of memory in the second dynamic memory pool. The memory in this pool is used to keep track of open files, file locks and record locks.

Dynamic Memory 2: Peak Used. This gives the greatest amount of memory from the second pool in use at the same time since the server was last brought up.

Dynamic Memory 2: Currently in Use. This shows the amount of memory in the second pool currently in use.

Dynamic Memory 3: Maximum. This is the total amount of memory allocated to the third dynamic memory pool. This memory is used to track file server and routing information.

Dynamic Memory 3: Peak Used. This gives the greatest amount of memory from the third memory pool in use simultaneously since the server was last brought up.

Dynamic Memory 3: Currently in Use. This is the amount of memory in the third pool currently in use.

Volume Information   This option allows you to view specific information about each of the volumes (partitions) on your hard drive. If your drive has more than one volume, you have a window listing each of the volumes. Highlight the volume you want to investigate and press Enter. The following information appears:

Volume Name. This gives the name of the volume you have selected.

Volume Number. This is the number which was given to the volume.

Volume Mounted. This tells if the volume was brought into service when the file server was brought up.

Volume Removable. This shows if volume is removable. If the volume is removable, it can be mounted and dismounted while the file server is running. If it is not, it will only be dismounted if the hard drive fails. See Chapter 9 for information on Mount and Dismount.

Volume Hashed. This indicates if the volume is hashed. When a volume is hashed the system indexes the directories in each volume and then indexes the files by volume and subdirectory. This method of keeping track of directories, subdirectories, and files increases the speed with which files are accessed and maximizes network performance. Hashing is automatically done by the system unless it is short of memory.

Volume Cached. This shows if the volume is cached. This is determined during installation. It is advisable to cache because it speeds up network performance by keeping the volume directory entries in memory. As with hashing, if the server is short on memory it does not cache.

Block Size. This is the block size on the current volume.

Starting Block. This gives the block on the disk where the volume begins.

Total Blocks. This shows how many blocks are installed on the volume. This was determined during installation.

Free Blocks. This tells how many blocks are free and can be used in the volume.

Maximum Directory Entries. This is the highest number of directories, files, salvage files, and trustee entries that can exist on the volume.

Peak Directory Entries Used. This is the highest number of the directory entry that is being used by the volume.

Current Free Directory Entries. This shows how many directory entries are available for use. If you receive an "Access Denied" message when trying to create a directory or save a file, and you have trustee rights that allow you to perform the function, use Volinfo or Chkvol to check the current directory entries that are available.

Logical Drive Number. This is the logical number of the hard drive on the volume you selected.

Volume Mirrored. This tells if the drive is mirrored. When a drive is mirrored, two physical drives exist. Both drives contain exactly the same information. If one drive fails, the other takes over.

Primary Disk Number. This is the number of the physical disk the volume is stored on.

Mirror Disk Number. This is the number of the physical disk the volume is mirrored on.

Status

The Status screen gives the current server date and time, whether or not user login is enabled or transaction tracking is available. You can change the information on this screen. Just highlight the information to be changed, press Enter and type in the new information.

Version Information

The Version Information screen shows what version of Novell NetWare is used on your system.

VOLINFO

Volinfo is a command line utility. With it you can find the following information: the total disk storage space (in kilobytes), the amount of unused disk space, the total number of directory entries permitted, and the number of directory entries still free. To access this information, type Volinfo at the DOS prompt. You now have a screen listing each volume on the server with this information. You can also use Volinfo to change servers and to see volume information on another server. If you are running out of directory entries, you must either Purge (see Chapter 1 under Command Line Utilities) or rerun Netgen and increase the number of directory entries. (See your Novell manual for more information on Netgen.)

CHKVOL

You can also use Chkvol to find the amount of free space (in bytes) and free directories entries on one specific volume. To see this information about the current volume, type CHKVOL and press Enter at the DOS prompt. To get information about a volume that is not currently selected, type CHKVOL and the volume number on which you need this information (e.g., CHKVOL SYS2: and press Enter).

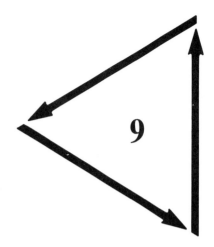

9

Monitoring through the Console

THE console is the CRT screen and keyboard attached to the file server. Commands entered at the console enable you to monitor the various file server activities. There are also many printer commands you can enter from the console. These commands are listed separately at the end of this chapter. The commands are listed alphabetically.

NONPRINTER CONSOLE COMMANDS

Broadcast

Syntax   BROADCAST [*message*]

Purpose   This command is used to send messages to every workstation logged on to or attached to the file server. You can also send messages through the Novell menu utility Fconsole. For further information on Fconsole, see Chapter 8. See also, Send.

Clear Message

Syntax   CLEAR MESSAGE

Purpose   This command permits you to clear messages that have been sent to the console without clearing the rest of the screen.

Clear Station

Syntax   CLEAR STATION [*n*]

where *n* is a number.

Purpose   This command is used when a workstation has "frozen" or "crashed". It closes all of the open files and is equivalent to a user "logout."

Config

Syntax   CONFIG

Purpose   This command shows you the hardware configuration of the network file server.

Console

Syntax   CONSOLE

Purpose   This command switches a non-dedicated filer server from DOS to the console mode. See also, DOS.

Disable Login

Syntax   DISABLE LOGIN

Purpose   This command is used to prevent users from logging on to the file server. If a user has already logged on, he is able to continue working on the server until he logs out. Therefore, if you use this command because you are going to bring the server down, issue a message to all users currently logged in. See also, Enable Login.

Disk

Syntax   DISK

Purpose   The DISK command permits you to see the status and statistics of the network disk drives.

Dismount

Syntax   DISMOUNT [*pack*] [*volume number*]

Purpose   This command is used to remove a movable volume from the file server. See also, Mount.

DOS

Syntax   DOS

Purpose   This command switches a non-dedicated file server from the console mode into DOS. See also, Console.

Down

Syntax   DOWN

Purpose   This command shuts down the Novell operating system. In order to bring the system back up you have to reboot.

Enable Login

Syntax   ENABLE LOGIN

Purpose   This command reverses the effects of the Disable Login command and permits users to log on to the file server. See also, Disable Login.

Monitor

Syntax   MONITOR [*station number*]

Purpose   This command brings up the Monitor display that shows all workstations connected to the server and the activity at each station. When used without the station number, Monitor shows information for the first six workstations. To view additional work stations, you must specify the station number.

Mount

Syntax   MOUNT [*pack*] [*volume number*]

Purpose   This command adds a removable volume to the server.

Name

Syntax   NAME

Purpose   This command displays the name of the file server currently in use.

Off

Syntax   OFF

Purpose   This command clears the console screen.

Remirror

Syntax   REMIRROR [*n*]

where *n* is the number of the specified drive.

Purpose   This command is used to restart mirroring or duplexing for a specified drive. See also, Unmirror.

Send

Syntax   SEND "*message*" [*to*] [*station numbers*]
             (NOTE: The message must be enclosed in quotes)

Purpose   This command permits you to send console messages to specified stations. See also, Broadcast in this chapter and Fconsole in Chapter 8.

Set Time

Syntax   SET TIME [*month/day/year*] [*hour:minute:second*]

Purpose   This command sets the time and/or the date on the file server. See also, Time in this chapter and Fconsole, status in Chapter 8.

Time

Syntax   TIME

Purpose   This command displays the time and date on the file server. See also Set Time in this chapter and Fconsole, Status in Chapter 8.

Unmirror

Syntax   UNMIRROR [*n*]

where *n* is the number of the specified drive.

Purpose   This command shuts down the mirroring feature of a specified drive. See also Remirror and Chapter 8.

Vap

Syntax   VAP

Purpose   This command shows you a list of all value-added processes and their commands currently loaded onto the system.

PRINTER CONSOLE COMMANDS

Add Queue to Printer

Syntax   P[RINTER] [*n*] *ADD* [QUEUE] [*name*] [[AT] [PRIORITY] n]

Purpose   This command adds an existing queue to a printer or reroutes a queue from one printer to another. See also, Create New Print Queue, Change Queue Priority and Delete Queue from Printer.

Change Form Type Mounted in Printer

Syntax   P[RINTER] [*n*] *FORM* [*x*]

where *n* is the printer number and *x* is the form number.

Purpose   This command tells the server that you have changed the type of paper in the printer. See also, Chapter 7, Printers.

Change Queue Priority

Syntax   Q[UEUE] [*name*] C[HANGE] [JOB] [*n*] [TO] [PRIORITY] [*x*]
where n is the print job and x is the priority number.

Purpose   This command moves a print job from one position in the queue to another. See also, List Queue Contents.

Change Spooler Mapping

Syntax   S[POOL] *n* [TO] [QUEUE] [*name*]

Purpose   This command redirects the queue to which all print jobs for the specified spooler are sent. See also, List Current Spooler Mappings.

Create New Print Queue

Syntax   Q[UEUE] [*name*] CREATE

Purpose   This command creates a new print queue. It also gives the group Everyone rights to use the queue, gives the supervisor operator rights to the queue, and gives the file server rights to service the queue. You must also assign a spooler to a new queue. See also Spool and Change Spooler Mapping in this chapter and Chapter 7, Printers.

Delete All Jobs in Queue

Syntax   Q[QUEUE] [*name*] D[EL[ETE]] [JOB] *

Purpose   This command deletes all jobs listed in a specified queue. See also, Delete Queue Job, Delete Queue from Printer, List Queue Contents, Destroy Print Queue.

Delete Queue from Printer

Syntax   P[RINTER] [*n*] DEL[ETE] [QUEUE] [*name*]
where *n* is the printer number.

Purpose   This command temporarily removes a queue from the printer. See also, Add Queue to Printer.

Delete Queue Job

Syntax   *Q*[UEUE] [*name*] *D*[EL[ETE]] [JOB] [*x*]

Purpose   This command deletes a specific job from a specified print queue. See also, Delete All Jobs in Queue and List Queue Contents.

Destroy Print Queue

Syntax   *Q*[UEUE] [*name*] *DESTROY*

Purpose   This command destroys a print queue as well as all the jobs in it. See also, Delete All Jobs in Queue, Delete Queue from Printer and Add Queue to Printer.

Form Feed

Syntax   *P*[RINTER [*n*] *FF*

Purpose   This command advances the paper in the printer by one page. See also, Mark Top of Form.

List a Printer's Queue

Syntax   *P*[RINTER] [*n*] [*Q*[QUEUE[S]]]

Purpose   This command lists all of the queues being serviced by a specific printer. See also, List All Print Queues and List Queue Contents.

List All Print Queues

Syntax   *Q*[UEUE[S]]

Purpose   This command lists all of the print queues serviced by a file server. See also, List a Printer's Queues and List Queue Contents.

List Current Spooler Mappings

Syntax   *S*[POOL]

Purpose   This command displays the current spooler mappings for the server. For further information, refer to Chapter 7, "Printers." See also, Change Spooler Mapping.

List Printer Status

Syntax   *P*[RINTER[S]]

Purpose   This command lists information about all of the printers that are attached to the server. See also, List a Printer's Queues and List All Print Queues.

List Queue Contents

Syntax   *Q*[UEUE] [*name*] [JOB[S]]

Purpose   This command lists all of the print jobs in a printer's queue. See also, Change Queue Priority.

Mark Top of Form

Syntax   *P*[RINTER] [*n*] *MARK* [[TOP OF] FORM]

Purpose   This command prints a row of asterisks to indicate where on the page the printing will start. See also, Form Feed.

Rewind Printer

Syntax   *P*[RINTER] [*n*] *REWIND* [*x*] [PAGES]

Purpose   This command rewinds the current print job a specified number of pages and then resumes printing at that point. If you do not specify the number of pages, printing starts at the beginning of the job. See also, Start Printer and Stop Printer.

Start Printer

Syntax   *P*[RINTER] [*n*] *START*

Purpose   This command reverses the effect of the STOP PRINTER command and restarts the printer. See also, Stop Printer.

Stop Printer

Syntax   *P*[RINTER] [*n*] *STOP*

Purpose   This command temporarily stops a printer. To restart it, you must use the Start Printer command.

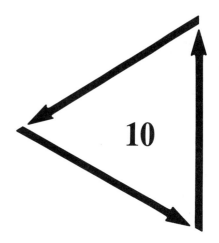

10

Troubleshooting

GIVEN the complexity of a network, it is not surprising that problems occur. Tracking down the source of the problem and finding a solution can be a frustrating experience. No wonder the supervisor often has to overcome the temptation to approach troubleshooting by shooting the element responsible for the trouble.

Network problems can be broken down into three major categories: hardware failure; operating system failure; or applications interface failure. To complicate the issue even further, problems frequently involve more than one category. The process of keeping the system running and minimizing the damage, in spite of failure in any of the above categories is called fault tolerance. SFT (Software Fault Tolerant) NetWare has built-in features that automatically correct certain problems as they occur on a network. For example, NetWare's HotFix feature prevents data from being stored on a damaged sector of a hard disk. However, problems that cannot be corrected directly by NetWare must be dealt with by the supervisor.

This chapter covers some of the more common problems encountered on a network. In it we detail what action should be taken to resolve the problem. We also suggest preventative measures, particularly on the hardware level, to avoid these problems in the first place.

SOME PREVENTATIVE MEASURES

One of the most common disasters on a network is data loss, either through hardware failure, software failure, or user error. There are several measures which you can use to prevent this problem from occurring.

Uninterrupted Power Supply

Power fluctuation or complete power loss frequently cause lost data or even damage to the hardware. This problem can be minimized by using an Uninterrupted Power Supply (UPS). A UPS will continue to supply power to the system for a designated time period, even if there is a complete power failure. The time they will give allows the users on the network to save their data and log out. SFT NetWare will also support monitoring boards that come with some UPS's. These interface with the terminals to warn users that the system is being taken down so they can log out immediately. Many excellent UPS devices are on the market. Almost all are compatible with Novell.

Duplexing

Duplexing is a means of storing all information on two hard drives at the same time, each drive operating off its own controller. This means that if one hard drive fails, the other will continue to be in operation. Because hard drive damage or failure is one of the most common causes of data loss, duplexing is an excellent means of solving the problem. The chance that both drives and the controller board will go bad at the same time are extremely small.

Tape Backup System

Backing up data from the hard drive regularly is the single most important method of avoiding data loss. A tape backup system is the best way to back up all data on the file server. This is usually handled on a rotation basis, with a different volume being backed up every night, while the system is not being used for anything else. Duplicate sets of the back up tapes should be made. At least one set of tapes should be stored at another location. This way, in the event of fire, water damage or theft, the data is safe and can be restored. The tapes can also be used to restore accidentally deleted files if the system has been shut down since the deletion and other utilities cannot restore the file. There are many different tape backup systems on the market that work well with Novell.

PREVENTING DATA LOSS THROUGH APPLICATIONS

Many software programs (such as WordPerfect) come equipped with their own temporary backup feature. By utilizing these features, data can be restored in the event of a power failure or keyboard lockup.

BINDERY PROBLEMS

Many problems can occur on a network when the bindery files containing the user information become corrupted. If any of the following problems occur, it probably means that your bindery files require repair:

- A CANNOT EXECUTE MENUPARZ.EXE prompt occurs when a user logs in.

- User names cannot be deleted or modified.

- User passwords cannot be changed.

- User rights cannot be modified.

- UNKNOWN SERVER appears when attempting to print.

- BINDERY console errors occur during any Novell application.

The bindery consists of two files: NET$BIND.SYS and NET$ BVAL.SYS. The files contain network information about users, user groups, queues and account charge rates.

Running Bindfix can correct most bindery file problems. Bindfix shuts down the bindery files, makes copies of them (using the same file name with an .OLD extension), scans the bindery files for problems and attempts to correct them. When Bindfix has completed its tasks you will be notified by the utility as to whether or not the bindery check was successful. If Bindfix fails, or if there is a power failure while you are running it, running Bindrest will restore the .OLD versions of the files. In order to run Bindfix or Bindrest follow these steps:

1. From the DOS prompt, go to volume SYS:.

2. When in the SYS: volume, change to the SYSTEM directory.

3. At the SYS:SYSTEM DOS prompt, type:

BINDFIX (BINDREST)

Bindfix attempts to correct any problems or damage to the bindery files. You will be asked whether or not you want to have obsolete mail directories or users deleted. If you answer Yes, Bindfix will delete these old files.

PROBLEMS OPENING FILES, COPYING FILES, AND WRITING TO DISK

The following problems can occur during the process of copying files or writing to disk:

Access Denied

An Access Denied message usually means that the user has insufficient trustee writes to open a file or write to the file. It can also mean that the volume you are working in has run out of directory entries and it is necessary to either Purge (see Chapter 1) or rerun Netgen (see the Novell manual). This problem can usually be avoided, if the person who installed the program set the system for the maximum number of directory entries.

Disk I/O Read Error

When you get a Disk I/O Error message, it means there is not enough memory left in the file server to process the request, or that there is a hardware problem with the file server (probably the hard drive, controller card, or one of the memory chips is damaged).

Failed to Create File

The Failed to Create File message indicates that a user tried to copy a file to another file that is currently being used or is flagged as Read-Only. To correct the problem, wait until the other user is finished with the file or have him close the file. If the file is flagged Read-Only, have someone with Parental rights in the directory change the flag.

Failed to Open File *filename*

A Failed to Open File message is generated when a user tries to copy a file currently in use by someone else. It can also appear when the file is flagged as Read-Only. To correct the problem, wait until the other user is finished with the file or have him close the file. If the file is flagged Read-Only, have someone with Parental rights in the directory change the flag.

Fatal Copy Error Writing to Disk

You get a Fatal Copy Error Writing to Disk message when you try to write a file to a damaged local disk. If you are using a hard disk, back up the data and reformat the disk (a physical format may be necessary if the problem persists); if you are using a floppy disk, copy all the existing data and throw out the bad disk.

Insufficient Disk Space to Write

The Insufficient Space to Write problem can occur when writing to the network hard drive. There are two main causes: The current volume is filled to capacity; or the user's available space, limited by the supervisor in the Syscon Accounting feature, is full. To solve the problem, delete files in the volume to clear up space, write to a different volume or increase the users' available space.

Insufficient Space on Backup Disk

You can get the Insufficient Space on Backup Disk for two reasons. The obvious one is that there is not enough room left on the disk you are trying to back up to. The problem can also occur, however, while inside an application (such as WordPerfect) while trying to back up files to a directory which has not been mapped. If this happens, map the backup directory. You must ensure that a search map has also been created in the Login Script for the path containing the program execute file. See Chapter 4 for information on Login Scripts.

Memory Allocation Table Full

Getting a Memory Allocation Table Full message means you do not have enough memory available to run your application. It frequently occurs when too many TSR (terminate and stay resident) programs are being used. If it occurs during an application or applications that you have run before without difficulty, it may be that some of the memory chips in the local terminal are damaged. To solve the problem, reboot the terminal and run the application again. If the problem still occurs, you may have to remove the TSR program(s) or purchase additional memory.

Missing or Invalid Command Interpreter

You get the Missing or Invalid Command Interpreter message when exiting an application. It means that Novell is unable to locate the DOS

COMMAND.COM file. To solve the problem insert the following command in the System Login Script:

```
MAP Sn:=SYSn:DOS
COMSPEC=Sn:COMMAND.COM
```

Where *n* is a variable number defining the search path and volume. (See Chapter 4 for mapping information.)

Users Are Accessing Blank Directories

If a user has not been assigned trustee rights to a directory, but tries to access it anyway, it will appear to be blank and the user cannot access any of the files in it.

Users Are Being Logged Out of the Network or Not Allowed to Log On

Check to be sure the account balance for these users has not been used up. (See Chapter 5, Security and Supervisor Options, Accounting.)

PRINTING PROBLEMS

Printer problems are probably the most common problems on a network. Because print jobs involve software applications, the network operating system, and the output device (printer or plotter), the chance for errors is immense and tracking the problem can be very difficult. This section lists some of the more common printing problems we have encountered and how we deal with them.

The most common problem is sending a print job and it does not print. The first step in dealing with this problem is to determine where the cause of the problem is. Is it in the software application, the network operating system, a hardware problem (such as a bad cable), or a printer problem.

1. If your application software is capable of reporting print job status, check and see if the job is being held up at the application level and why. If it is being held up at this level, correct the problem, delete the job from the queue and send it again.

2. If your application software is not capable of reporting print job status or if the job has already been sent from the software to Novell, use Pconsole to see if the job is in the queue. If it is, delete it. If it is not, then there is a problem with transmission from your

software application to Novell. See Chapter 7 for more information on Pconsole.

3. Try printing from another software application on the system. If you have no trouble with print jobs sent from another software application to the same printer, you can assume that the problem is not with the printer.

4. The next step is to go back into the original software application and send another job to the printer.

5. Ensure you have selected the correct printer in the software. If this is alright, next verify that the software application can recognize a network printer (even some of the network application software packages do not). If the software does not recognize a network printer, you must reroute the local printer to a network printer (see chapter 7, Printers, Printing from the Command Line, Capture).

6. Capture the printer at the DOS prompt before you execute the software. Verify that you have selected the same local printer in your software, as the one you rerouted, and then send the job again.

7. If this does not work call the technical support number listed in the manual that came with your software.

The following error messages frequently appear when a printing problem occurs:

- FORM NAME DOES NOT EXIST—This message means you sent a print job and specified a form name that Novell cannot locate. Check to be certain that you typed the form name correctly. If you have and Novell still cannot locate the form, check Pconsole to be sure the form has been defined. (See chapter 7 for information on Pconsole.)

- INSUFFICIENT DISK SPACE TO CREATE A PRINT FILE— This message means you do not have enough free disk space left on the file server to route the print job to a temporary file on SYS:. Novell sends all print jobs to a temporary print file. The job is then routed to a printer, when one becomes available. When this message occurs, you must either delete files (to make more space available); or, if the supervisor has allocated a certain amount of space per user, the supervisor can increase the space allocated.

- MOUNT FORM nn—This is a console message. It means that a form has been chosen for a print job specifying a different type of paper. You must mount a new form at the file server console using the following syntax:

PRINTER *n* FORM *x*

where *n* is the printer number and *x* is the form number. The problem sometimes occurs while using certain software applications with network print drivers. It can be circumvented by selecting a local print driver in the software and then using Capture to reroute the local printer to a network printer at the DOS prompt.

OTHER PROBLEMS

- Newly Created Print Queue Does Not Work—You have created a new print queue and attached it to a printer. It does not work. The most common reason it does not work, is that you didn't assign a spooler to it. When you create a new queue, you must first attach it to a printer and then assign a spooler to it. (For more detailed information, see Chapter 5 for information on Edit System Autoexec File, and Chapter 7 on Printers.)

- A printer suddenly stops printing jobs from one terminal—Everyone is sending jobs to be printed with no problem. Suddenly, the print jobs sent by one terminal are no longer being printed. What to do? First, check Pconsole and delete all jobs from the queue. Then send a job from the terminal. If that does not work, delete all jobs from the queue, turn the printer off and down the server. This is a nuisance, but printing for the problem terminal is usually restored when the file server is brought back up.

Index

> redirection symbol, xvi
[ ] square brackets, variables, xv
| piping symbol, xv

A

Access Denied message, 222
account balances, charge rates,
   130-131
accounting option, 5, 17
   account restrictions, 110-113, 110
   audits, 18
   charge rates, 125
   deactivate, 128
   delete server, 127
   installation, 126
   reports, 125-126
   Syscon menu utility, 125-126
archived files, 28
Atotal, 17
Attach, 20, 97-98
audits, 18
AUTOEXEC.SYS file, editing,
   security, 119-121

B

backup files, 28, 223
   hard disk partitions, 37-38
   tape backup systems, 141, 220
banners, printing and printers, 177
bindery files, 17, 19, 221-222
Bindfix, 17
Bindrest, 17
Break, 98
Broadcast, 211

C

cache statistics, 198-200
Capture, 20, 182-185
Castoff, 20
Caston, 21
channel statistics, 200
charge rates, 125, 128-129
   account balances, 130-131
   calculating, 129
   changing, 129

Chkvol, 21, 209
Clear Message, 211-212
Clear Station, 212
color selections, 1, 9-11, 149-151
Colorpal menu utility, 1, 9-11
Command Interpreter, 223-224
command line utilities, 16-33, 74-76
   supervisor-only, 17-19
   user command line utility, 19-33
COMMAND.COM, 88, 223-224
commands, xiv
Comspec, 98-99
concurrent connections, 111
conditional command execution,
   If...Then, 102-105
Config, 212
confirmation boxes, menu utility, 3-4
consoles
   clear screen, 214
   Console command, 212
   monitoring through, 211-218
   nonprinter console commands,
     211-215
   printer console commands, 215-218
conventions, commands, xiv-xvi

D

date and time stamps, 32
   directories and subdirectories, 48
   servers, 214-215
   System Login scripts, 86-87
directories and subdirectories, 8, 9,
   25, 27, 42-45
   access rights control, 43
   attributes, 22
   blank, 224
   change current, 42
   create, 40, 46-48
   date and time stamps, 48
   delete, 46-48
   exclude pattern, 57
   hard disks, 36-41
   include pattern, 58
   list, 23
   LOGIN, 77

MAIL, 77
owners, 44, 50
PUBLIC, 77, 134, 149
purging files, 29
rename, 30, 48
SYSTEM, 77, 125
trustee rights, 32, 44-45, 50-52, 72
Disable Login, 212
Disk, 212
Disk I/O Error message, 222
disk mapping statistics, 200
disk resource limitations, security,
   113
disk statistics, 200-201
Dismount, 213
Display, 99
DOS, 213
   environment settings, 99-100
   interrupt commands, 99
   menu access from, 146
   verify data copy to drives, 100
DOS Break On/DOS Break Off, 99
DOS Set, 99-100
DOS Verify, 100
Down, 213
Drive, 100-101
drivers, device, information about,
   29, 197, 198
drives
   default selection, 8, 100-101
   duplexing or mirroring, 214-215
   mapped, 8, 24, 79-80, 95-97,
     106-107
   mirroring or duplexing, 214-215
   search drives, 8, 80-81, 98-99
   status and statistics, 212
duplexing, 214-215, 220

E

e-mail, 77
Enable Login, 213
Endcap, 21, 185-186
equivalences, user security, 114
error logs, 124
error messages, menus, 151-153

execute-only files, 26, 61, 73
Exit, 101
expiration dates, accounts, 111
External Program Execution (#),
    101-102

F

Fatal Copy Error, 223
Fconsole menu utility, 189-208
    broadcast messages, 190-191, 193
    clear connections, 193
    driver information, 197, 198
    file/lock activity, 196, 197
    LAN drive information, 197, 198
    logical record locks, 194
    open files, 194-196
    purge files, 198
    semaphores, 196
    servers, change current, 191-192
    servers, connection information,
        192-196
    servers, down, 196
    statistics, 198-207
    task information, 196
    usage statistics, 196
Fdisplay, 99
file servers (*see* servers)
Filer menu utility, 1, 8-9, 41-58
    attributes, 54-55
    copying files, 55-56
    current directory, 8, 9, 42
    current directory, access rights
        control, 43
    current directory, owner, 44
    current directory, trustee rights,
        44-45
    default settings, 56-58
    delete files, 52-54, 56
    directories and subdirectories,
        42-45
    directories, exclude pattern, 57
    directories, include pattern, 58
    file information, 8
    history of files, 56
    include/exclude files, 58
    option setting, 9
    overwrite files, 56-57
    rename files, 52-54
    search attributes, 58
    subdirectories, 9

subdirectories, access rights
    control, 49-50
subdirectories, create/delete, 46-48
subdirectories, date and time, 48
subdirectories, exclude pattern, 57
subdirectories, include pattern, 58
subdirectories, owner, 50
subdirectories, rename, 48
subdirectories, trustee rights, 50-52
trustee rights, 61
volume information, 9, 42
files
    Access Denied, 222
    activity monitoring, 196, 197
    archived, 28
    attributes, 8-9, 18, 19, 21-22, 26,
        54-55, 61, 72-74
    backups, 28, 223
    copying, 24, 55, 56
    create, 72, 222
    dates, 25-26
    delete, 8-9, 56, 52-54, 72
    directories and subdirectories, 8, 9,
        27, 224
    Disk I/O Error message, 222
    execute-only, 26, 61, 73
    Fatal Copy Error, 223
    hidden, 18, 19, 26, 58, 61, 73
    history, 56
    include/exclude from directory list,
        58
    indexed, 26, 61, 73
    information, 24-28
    Macintosh, 27
    Memory Allocation Table Full
        message, 223
    Missing/Invalid Command
        Interpreter, 223-224
    modified, 26, 61, 73
    names, 25
    open, 72, 194-196, 222
    overwrite, 56-57
    problems and troubleshooting,
        222-224
    protected, 18
    purging, 29, 198
    read, 71
    read-only, 26, 61, 73
    read-write, 26, 61, 73
    recover, 30

rename, 8-9, 52-54
search attributes, 58, 72
security, 22-23
sharing, 26, 61, 73
size, 26, 27, 223
sorting, 27
statistics, 201-203
system, 26, 58, 61, 73
transactional, 26, 61, 73
updates, 25, 27
volume information, 9
wildcards, 25
write, 71
Fire Phasers, 102
Flag, 21, 74
Flagdir, 22
form feeds, printing and printers, 177

G

game, Nsnipes, 29
grace logins, 112
Grant, 22, 74
groups, 5, 33, 59
    adding, Syscon, 64-65
    assign trustee rights, 66-68
    deleting, Syscon, 64-65
    grant trustee rights, 22, 66-68, 74,
        75
    hard disk partitions, 37-41
    list, 8
    remove trustee rights, 30, 76
    revoke trustee rights, 30, 76
    security, 113

H

hard drive organization, 35-58
    directories, 36-41
    disk resource limitation, security,
        113
    Filer menu utility, 41-58
    networking concepts, 35-36
    partitioning, 36-41
Help menu utility, 2
hidden files, 18, 19, 26, 58, 61, 73
Hidefile, 18
history of file (*see* files, history)
Holdoff, 22
Holdon, 23
horizontal menu placement, 148
hot fix function, 201

I

I/O statistics, LANs, 203-204
If...Then, 102-105
Include, 105
indexed files, 26, 61, 73
information entry boxes, menu utility, 3-4
intruder detection/lockout status, security, 113, 123-124
Ipx driver, information about, 29

K

keywords, Makeuser menu utility, 13-15

L

LAN driver, information about, 29, 197, 198
Listdir, 23
local area networks (LAN), x-xi
 I/O statistics, 203-204
 driver device, information about, 29, 197-198
locks, 196, 197
logical record locks, 194
Login, 23
LOGIN directory, 77
Login scripts, 79-108, 114
 commands, 97-108
 conditional command execution (If...Then), 102-105
 connect file servers (Attach), 97-98
 default drives (Drive), 100-101
 display text files, 99
 DOS, environment settings (DOS Set), 99-100
 DOS, interrupt commands (DOS Break), 99
 DOS, verify data copy (DOS Verify), 100
 external program execution (#), 101-102
 machine name of station, 105-106
 mapped drives, 79-80
 mapped drives (Map command), 106-107
 menu access from, 146
 messages, 81
 messages, Write, 107-108
 multiple servers, 81-82

pause execution (Pause), 107
phaser sound effects (Fire Phasers), 102
print screen text files (Include), 105
remarks   (Remark), 107
search drive, 80-81, 98-99
stop execution (Break), 98
System, 82-89
terminate command execution (Exit), 101
User, 82-83, 89-95
Logout, 23, 141

M

Machine Name, 105-106
Macintosh files, 27
MAIL directory, 77
Makeuser command, 18, 75-76
Makeuser menu utility, 12-16, 18, 59
 keywords, 13-15
 sample sessions, 15-16
 USR files, 13
Map command, 24, 106-107
mapped drives, 8, 24, 79-80, 95-97, 106-107
 create, 95-97
 delete, 95-97
 editing, 95-97
 reusing, 145
 Session menu utility, 95-97
 statistics, 200
 System Login scripts, 87-88
Memory Allocation Table, full message, 223
memory usage
 hard disk partitions, 37-41
 Memory Allocation Table, 223
Menu menu utility, 1, 2, 12, 133-153
 color selections, 149-151
 DOS access, 146
 error messages, 151-153
 files necessary, 134
 Forms submenu, 143-144
 horizontal placement, 148
 Login script access, 146
 main menu text file, 135-145
 mapped drives, reuse, 145
 menu application and use, 133-134
 PUBLIC directory, 134
 Sales submenu, 144-145

text files, saving, 145
user menu creation, 134-146
variables, 147
vertical placement, 147-148
WordPerfect submenu, 142-143
menu utilities, 1-16
 accessing, 2
 Colorpal, 1, 9-11
 confirmation boxes, 3-4
 exiting, 4
 Filer, 1, 8-9
 Help feature, 2
 information entry boxes, 3-4
 Makeuser, 12-16, 18
 Menu, 1, 2, 12
 option selections, 2
 Pconsole, 1, 12
 Printcon, 1, 10-11
 Printdef, 1, 10-11
 Session, 1, 7-8
 submenus, 3-4
 Syscon, 1, 5-7
 Volinfo, 1, 9-10
messages
 broadcast, 190-191, 193, 211
 clear, 211-212, 211
 Login scripts, 81
 re-enable, 21
 sending, 31, 214
 suppression, 20
 System Login scripts, 85-87
 Write command, Login scripts, 107-108
mirroring, 214-215
modes, print devices, 161-163
modified files, 26, 61, 73
Monitor, 213
monitoring activity
 console for, 211-218
 files, 196-197
 terminals for, 189-209
Mount, 214

N

Name, 214
Ncopy, 24
Ndir, 24
Netbios, information about, 29
networking, 35-36
Nprint, 28, 186-187

Nsnipes, 29
Nver, 29

O

Off, 214
operating systems
    information about, 29
    shut down, 213

P

palettes (*see* color selections)
parental rights, 72
partitioning hard disk, 36-41
passwords (*see also* security), 19, 31,
    111-113
Paudit, 18
Pause, 107
pause for data entry, System Login
    scripts, 87
Pconsole menu utility, 1, 12, 172-182
phaser sound effects, 85, 102
piping, xv
Printcon menu utility, 1, 10-11,
    166-172
Printdef menu utility, 1, 10-11,
    157-161
printers (*see* printing and printers)
printing and printers, 155-187,
    224-226
    attach file server, 172-173
    banners, 177
    cancel, 178
    Capture command, 182-185
    change user name on attached
        server, 173-174
    command line printing, 182-187
    configuring print jobs, 10
    configuring print jobs, copying,
        171-172
    configuring print jobs, default, 171
    configuring print jobs, delete, 170
    configuring print jobs, edit,
        170-171
    configuring print jobs, Printcon,
        166-172
    configuring print jobs, rename, 170
    copies, number of, 176
    copying definitions/modes between
        file servers, 163-166
    define printer functions, 10
    detach file server, 173

Endcap command, 185-186
form feeds, 177, 217
forms definitions, paper type,
    165-166, 215
modes, print devices, 161-163
Nprint, 186-187
paper type, 165-166, 215
parameters, 176-178
pause print job, 176
Pconsole menu utility, 12, 172
Printcon feature, 166-172
Printdef feature, 157-161
printer console commands, 215-218
printer status, 29, 218
problems and troubleshooting,
    224-226
queues, 155-156, 174
queues, add, 174-178, 215
queues, cancel print job, 178
queues, change parameters, 178
queues, contents, 218
queues, create, 182, 216
queues, delete all jobs, 182, 216
queues, delete specified job, 182,
    216-217
queues, destroy, 217
queues, hold, 176
queues, list, 174, 181, 217
queues, priority, 176, 179, 216
queues, servers, view, 180
queues, view and print status,
    179-180
redirect, 20, 182-185
rewind job to specified page, 218
send file to printer (Nprint), 28,
    186-187
servers, full name, 181
servers, ID, 181
servers, list, 181
servers, view, 180
sharing printers, 155-156
spoolers, 216, 217
start printer, 218
stop printer, 218
tabs, 177
targeting output, 177
terminate capture process, 21,
    185-186
text vs. byte stream, 176
value-added processes, 157

prompts, System Login scripts, 88-89
protected files, 18
Pstat, 29
PUBLIC directory, 77, 134, 149
Purge, 29

Q

queues, printing, 155-156, 174
    add, 174-178, 215
    cancel print job, 178
    change parameters, 178
    contents, 218
    create, 182, 216
    delete all jobs, 182, 216
    delete specified job, 182, 216-217
    destroy, 217
    hold, 176
    list, 174, 181, 217
    priority, 176, 179, 216
    servers, view, 180
    view and print status, 179-180

R

read-only files, 26, 61, 73
read-write files, 26, 61, 73
redirection, xvi
Remark, 107
Remirror, 214
Remove, 30, 76
Rendir, 30
reports, accounting, 125-126
Revoke, 30, 76
Rights, 30

S

Salvage, 30
search drives, 8, 80-81, 98-99
    create, 97
    delete, 97
    editing, 97
    Session menu utility, 97
searches
    search attributes, files, 58
    search drives, 8, 80-81, 98-99
    search mode, 31-32, 31
    search paths, System Login scripts,
        88
    trustee rights, 72
Security command, 19
security, 22-23, 30, 33, 109-132

account balances, 117, 110-113, 130-131

account restrictions, 110-113, 117, 130-131

accounting option, deactivate, 128

accounting option, delete server, 127

accounting option, installation, 126-127

accounting option, Syscon, 125

accounting reports, 125-126

AUTOEXEC.SYS file, edit, 119-121

charge rates, 125, 128-129

concurrent connections, 111

directories and subdirectories, 43, 49-50

disk resource limitation, 113

error logs, 124

expiration dates, 111

file server console operators status, 121-122

file/lock activity, 196, 197

full-name of user option, 113

grace logins, 112

groups, 113

intruder detection/lockout, 113, 123-124

logical record locks, 194

login scripts, 114

passwords, 111, 112, 113

security equivalences, 114

station restrictions, 115

supervisor options, 117-124

System Login script, 124

time restrictions, 115-119

trustee rights, 62, 117

users, 109-117

semaphores, 196

Send, 31, 214

servers, 33
    access, Login, 23
    add volume, 214
    broadcast messages, 193
    change current server, 5, 7-8, 191-192
    clear connection, 193
    configuration, 212
    connect to, 20, 97-98, 192-196
    connection information, 192-196

console operator status, 121-122

console to DOS mode, 213

copying print definitions/modes between, 163-166

date and time stamps, 214-215

DOS to console mode, 212

downing, 196

enable login, 213

error logs, 124

full name, printing and printers, 181

ID, printing and printers, 181

list, 31, 181

logical record locks, 194

Login scripts, multiple servers, 81-82

multiple, Login scripts and, 81-82

name, 214

prevent login, 212

remove volume, 213

terminate connection, Logout, 24

view information, 5

Session menu utility, 1, 7-8, 95-97
    change current server, 7-8
    default drive selection, 8
    group lists, 8
    mapped drives, 8, 95-97
    search drives, 8, 97
    user list, 8

Set Time, 214

Setpass, 31

Setts, 31

shared files, 26, 61, 73

shells, information about, 29

Showfile, 19

Slist, 31

Smode, 31

sorting files, 27

sound effects, phasers, 85, 102

Spx driver, information about, 29

statistics, 198-207
    cache, 198-200
    channel, 200
    disk mapping informatin, 200
    disk, 200-201
    file system, 201-203
    hot fix function, 201
    LAN I/O , 203-204
    summary, system, 204-207
    usage, Fconsole menu utility, 196

volume, 207

subdirectories, 9
    access rights control, 49-50
    create/delete, 46-48
    date and time, 48
    exclude pattern, 57
    include pattern, 58
    owner, 50
    rename, 48
    trustee rights, 50-52

submenus, menu utility, 3-4

summary statistics, 204-207

supervisors
    command line utility, 17-19
    Syscon options, 5-6

Syscon menu utility, 1, 5-7, 59
    accounting option, 5, 125-126
    adding groups, 64-65
    adding users, 62-64
    change current server, 5
    deleting groups, 64-65
    deleting users, 62-64
    filer server information, 5
    group information, 5
    supervisor options, 5-6
    trustee rights, 61
    user information, 6

system date and time settings, 32

SYSTEM directory, 77, 125

system files, 26, 58, 61, 73

System Login scripts, 82-89
    command.com location, 88
    date and time, 86-87
    mapped drives, 87-88
    messages, 85-87
    pause for data entry, 87
    phaser sound effects, 85
    prompts, 88-89
    search paths, 88
    security, 124
    Supervisor options, 83

system statistics, 32, 204-207

Systime, 32

T

tabs, printing and printers, 177

tape backup systems, 141

targeting print output, 177

task information, Fconsole menu utility, 196

terminals, monitor/communicate
    through, 189-209
  Chkvol, 209
  Fconsole, 189-208
  Volinfo, 208
text files, saving, 145
Time, 215
time restrictions, security, 115-119
Tlist, 32
Transaction Tracking System (TTS),
    initialization, 31
transactional files, 26, 61, 73
troubleshooting, 219-226
trustee rights, 33, 60
  assigning, 60, 66-71, 117
  Create right, 72
  Delete right, 72
  directories and subdirectories,
    44-45, 50-52, 72
  Filer vs. Syscon, 61
  grant to user/groups, 22, 74, 75
  group assignment, 66-68
  hard disk partitions, 37-41
  list, 32
  Modify File Attribute right, 72
  Open right, 72
  Parental right, 72
  Read right, 71
  remove from user/groups, 30, 76
  revoke from user/groups, 30, 76

Search right, 72
system security, 62
user assignment, 68-71
Write right, 71
TSR programs, 101

U

uninterrupted power supply (UPS),
    220
Unmirror, 215
usage statistics, Fconsole menu utility,
    196
User Login scripts, 82-83, 89-95
Userlist, 32
users, 33, 59
  account balances, 130-131
  account restrictions, 110-113
  adding, Syscon, 62-64
  charge rates, 130-131
  command line utility, 19-33
  delete many simultaneously, 75-76
  deleting, Syscon, 62-64
  hard disk partitions, 37-41
  information about, Syscon menu
    utility, 6
  list, 8, 32
  make many simultaneously, 75-76
  remove trustee rights, 30, 76
  revoke trustee rights, 30, 76
  security equivalences, 114

security, 109-117
trustee rights assignment, 22, 74,
    68-71
User Login scripts, 89-95
User Login scripts, copying, 92-95
user-menu creation, 134-146
USR files, 13, 18, 75-76

V

value-added processes, 157, 215
Vap, 215
variables, xv, 147
vertical menu placement, 147-148
Volinfo menu utility, 1, 9-10, 208-209
volumes
  add, 214
  remove, 213
  space usage check, 21
  statistics, 207
  volume information, 9-10, 42

W

Whoami, 33
wildcards, file information, 25
WordPerfect submenu, 142-143
workstations
  display information/activity, 213
  frozen or crashed, 212
  restricting access, security, 115
Write, 107